TOXOPHILUS,

THE

SCHOLE, or PARTITIONS,

OF

SHOOTING.

Contayned in two Bookes.

ROGER ASCHAM

A facsimile reprint of the 1788 edition
with a new preface by E. G. Heath
Editor and Archivist to the Society of Archer-Antiquaries

Published by S.R. Publishers Ltd.
in collaboration with
The Society of Archer-Antiquaries
and
The Grand National Archery Society
1968

BIBLIOGRAPHIC NOTE

This edition is a facsimile reprint of the 1788 Wrexham edition printed by R. Marsh, with the inclusion of a new preface, the pagination of which is shown in parenthesis.

© S.R. PUBLISHERS LTD.
EAST ARDSLEY, WAKEFIELD, YORKSHIRE,
ENGLAND, 1968
S.B.N. 85409.536.5.

*Reprinted in Great Britain
by Redwood Press Limited,
Trowbridge, Wilts.*

PREFACE

In the summer of 1544 Roger Ascham, a reader in Greek at Cambridge who was to become tutor to Princess Elizabeth and the young Edward VI, announced that he had in press a book *de re Sagittaria* which he had dedicated to the King's majesty and which he hoped to present to Henry VIII before the royal departure for the wars in France. He hoped that the work would be "neither unworthy of my love for my country, nor an insignificant testimony of my inconsiderable learning". His confidence in this book was not misplaced and his hopes for its success were to be realised on a scale far greater than he could visualise. The first edition of *Toxophilus: the Schole of Shootinge Contayned in Two Bookes* was published by Edward Whitechurch in 1545 and very quickly became a standard work. Eminent authors, poets and playwrights for many years were to draw from it and large parts of the book were unashamedly reprinted without acknowledgement by writers such as Gervase Markham, Thomas Roberts, Shotterel and D'Urfey. To this day Ascham is quoted at length to illustrate shooting methods and to emphasise the more exacting aspects of the art of archery.

Apart from its subject matter, which merits careful study on its own account, Ascham presented *Toxophilus* as a specimen of a pure and correct English style, in the hope that the cultivation of the vernacular language by the scholars of the day would become as popular as the then exclusive study of Latin and Greek. The treatise, which is divided into two books, sets down the pleasant dialogue between two college Fellows, Philologus – lover of learning, and Toxophilus – lover of the bow, as they discourse beside the wheatfields in the neighbourhood of Cambridge throughout the long summer's afternoon, upon "the Booke and the Bowe". In the first book Toxophilus defends his love of archery by showing it to be the most honest and advantageous of exercises. He demonstrates, by citing numerous examples from modern and classical times, that all worthy nations have placed great value on archery because of its benefits in peace as well as in war. No other recreation is either so healthful or so proper for students. Its wholesomeness, its moderation, and the fact that it takes men out into the fresh air make it an ideal corrective for the temptation to spend their leisure hours in unlawful pastimes such as cards and dice. As ample proof that Toxophilus had by no means neglected his studies by pursuing his favourite sport, book one ends with a recitation of the many instances in which ancient peoples skilled in archery have won military renown. Philologus now declares that his interest is roused and asks his companion how a beginner can master so useful an art.

The second book, divided into two main sections, answers Philologus by dealing with everything that is necessary to achieve proficiency at shooting in a bow. Carefully explained are all the technical matters that an archer should know. Such items as the bracer, shooting glove, bow-string and bow and arrows are explained with loving care and the comparative merits of different materials and methods of construction are fully discussed with the confidence of an expert.

The book then deals with the techniques of shooting and it is here that Ascham's famous "five pointes" are patiently explained. After enumerating numerous faults and common errors Toxophilus admits that "of these faults I have very many myself". He then advises Philologus that "standyng, nocking, drawyng, holdyng and lowsyng, done as they should be done, make fayre shootyng". The final pages explain how the weather and other physical variables affect shooting and then thoughtful guidance is given regarding psychological problems which may manifest themselves, "all affectations and specially anger, hurteth both minde and body. The minde is blinde thereby: and if the minde be blinde, it cannot rule the body aright". The final words in the book belong to Philologus who, after expressing his complete satisfaction in the way Toxophilus has explained the intricacies of the ancient art of bowmanship, extends an invitation to his friend and teacher "nowe that the sunne is downe, therefore, if it please you, we will go home and drink together in my chamber, and there I will tell you plainly what I think of this communication, and also what we will appoint, at your request, for the other matter to meet here again". How many generations of archers since have followed this homely example by spending happy summer evenings discussing the day's archery over a glass of ale whilst making plans for further excursions into the unique world of toxophilitic delights.

What prompted Roger Ascham, the scholar in Latin and Greek, to emerge from the cloistered surroundings of dusty learning and write such a book? His practical motives were clearly twofold, financial benefit and a desire to promote himself in the world of scholarship. Undoubtedly he was also prompted by an irresistible urge to write about a subject of which he was very fond. We know he practised archery from an early age. During his life at Cambridge he suffered many disappointments in his career and this in turn affected his health. Searching for something to relax his mind and restore his bodily well-being he discovered a wonderful antidote in archery, his former love.

During the early part of the sixteenth century the longbow still occupied a place of honour and affection. It was still the pre-eminent weapon of recent memory. It had featured in the interminable wars between England and France and it was the "artillery" of the English armies so heavily relied on during the Wars of the Roses. Even more recently by its use the Scots had been routed at Flodden and again at Solway Moss. Henry VIII encouraged his subjects to practise their archery partly to stamp out "unlawful games that bred vice and effeminacy" and partly to maintain the longbow as a national arm. A competent bowman himself, he confirmed the statutes of Edward III which required every man and boy to own a longbow and to shoot regularly. Bishop Latimer, in a sermon before the young Edward VI, looked back with pride on the days when fathers gave their sons bows and supervised their shooting. "On Sundays" he recalled "men and boys were wont to go abroad in the fields a shooting; but now it is turned into glossing, gulling and whoring within the house".

There was obviously small risk that such a monarch as Henry VIII, in times when the bow still proved occasionally a more effective weapon than the gun and himself no mean exponent in the art, would scorn a book in commendation of archery. Ascham's tribute to this royal attitude was skilfully phrased and carefully timed: "Again, there is another thing, which above all other doth move me, not only to love shooting, to praise shooting, to exhort all others to shooting, but also to use shooting myself: and that is our King his most royal purpose and will, which in all his statutes generally doth command men, and with his own mouth most gently doth exhort men, and by his great gifts and rewards greatly doth encourage men, and with his most princely example very often doth provoke all other men to the same." The king accepted the book and was pleased to reward Ascham with a pension of £10 a year, which was not an inconsiderable sum in those days. Without doubt the name of Roger Ascham is legendary among archers of today who look upon him as their father-in-archery, he is quoted with respect and his instructions on how to shoot in a bow form a basic pattern which can still be followed.

In recent years archery as a sport has enjoyed a revival which has encouraged the use of modern materials and up-to-date methods of manufacture as well as a fresh look at shooting methods by experts who have made searching analyses into training and the techniques of using the bow and arrow. Much has been learnt in the technological field, performances with the bow have excelled even the wildest dreams of enthusiasts and archery has gained an admired place in international sport. Much of what Ascham wrote on the art of archery is as true today as it was when it was written more than 400 years ago, and the principles he laid down, although then applicable to the longbow, are, with little modification, of great practical value to the modern archer. That Roger Ascham was an archer there is no doubt; he felt deeply about his subject, as all true archers do, and encouraged others to follow suit by excellent instruction and praise hard to resist. Archery was to him "wholesome for the body, pleasant for the mind, comely for every man, worthy to be rebuked of no man, fit for all ages, persons and places".

The present edition, a reprint of the Wrexham, 1788, edition, dedicated to the Prince Regent who himself encouraged the eighteenth century revival of archery by his interest and patronage as well as by his personal example, will provide the means of acquiring a copy of the finest book on archery in English ever written. It is of fascinating interest as a focal point in the history of the bow for nearly five centuries and it is of inestimable value to the archer of today for its practical advice and sound toxophilitic lore.

E. G. Heath

TOXOPHILUS,

THE

SCHOLE, OR PARTITIONS,

OF

SHOOTING.

Contayned in II Bookes.

WRITTEN BY ROGER ASCHAM. 1544.
And now newlye perused.

Pleasaunt for all Gentlemen and Yomen of Englande. For theyr pastime to reade, and profitable for theyr use to folowe both in warre and peace.

ANNO 1571.

Imprinted at LONDON, in Fleteftreate, neare to Saint Dunstones Churche, by THOMAS MARSHE.

TO WHICH IS ADDED,

A

DEDICATION AND PREFACE,

BY THE REVEREND JOHN WALTERS, M. A.
Master of Ruthin School, and late Fellow of Jesus College, Oxford.

• • • • • • • • • • • • • •

WREXHAM:
REPRINTED BY R. MARSH.
MDCCLXXXVIII.

TO

HIS ROYAL HIGHNESS

THE

PRINCE of WALES,

PATRON,

OF THE INSTITUTION,

OF THE

ROYAL BRITISH BOWMEN;

THE

PRESIDENT AND MEMBERS OF THAT SOCIETY

PRESENT

THIS NEW EDITION OF

TOXOPHILUS,

AS A TESTIMONY OF THEIR WISHES FOR THE
REVIVAL OF ARCHERY, AND OF THEIR
ZEALOUS RESPECT, FOR THE
COUNTENANCE OF HIS
EXAMPLE AND HIS
PATRONAGE.

PREFACE.

THE reader who desires a circumstantial account of the following treatise and of its author, must be referred to the narration of his life in the Biographia Britannica, to Grant's publication of his Epistles, Upton's of his Schoolmaster, and Bennet's of his collected Works; the last of which is followed through this edition of Toxophilus. He will find in this place merely a few brief notices.

Roger Ascham was not simply a scholar and an author; he sustained also an active and an useful part in public life. In the reign of Henry VIII, when the Latin language bounded the attainments of scholars in this country, he taught Greek at Cambridge with dis-

b *tinguished*

tinguished reputation. An acquaintance with this elegant exotic was held in that age the principal accomplishment of female education, and Ascham was called from the university to teach the princesses and the ladies of the court to read Greek and to write a fine hand. Together with skill in caligraphy he possessed an exquisite Latin style, and with these qualifications held the place of Latin secretary to Edward VI, Mary I, and Elizabeth : having been the director of their studies, he became the vehicle of their politics. His memory claims the regard of his country, as that of one who was among the first institutors of Greek literature, and who, though not himself a reformer, was among the first friends of the reformation, in England.

Toxophilus, first published in 1544, was written at the university, purposely to recommend the exercise of the bow, as a salutary and liberal recreation, to the studious and sedentary. Like the Schoolmaster of the same author, it may justly be pronounced a consummate treatise. Apologetical and historical in the former, and

didactic

didactic in the latter, of the two books into which it is divided, it shrinks not from a comparison with any example of the discursive species of composition, of ancient or of modern date. By a revolution of times and manners, at once curious and perverse, these two admirable treatises have now changed hands, and each perhaps is studied most by that sex for which it was least intended. The bow, in the hands of the British fair, presents a new era in archery: without losing any thing of its effect, it has relaxed much of its stubbornness; to its ancient honours it has added novel and unexpected graces; it has struck out the unknown pleasure which the king of Persia sought in vain; and no longer exercised to wound and to destroy, bends to assimilate with the arts of peace, and forms a new link in the chain of society.

Some

Some Extracts from Books subfe-
quent to the date of Toxophilus.

" THERE died about three hundred, moſt
of them ſhot with arrows, which were reported to
be of the length of a taylor's yard; ſo ſtrong and
mighty a bow the Corniſhmen were ſaid to draw."

Lord Bacon's Hiſtory of the Reign of Henry VII.
p. 171. edit. 1641.

" At which day (of his coronation) he did in-
ſtitute for the better ſecurity of his perſon a band
of fifty archers, under a captain, to attend him,
by the name of yeomen of his guard."

Ibid. p. 10.

" What though with our 12,000 or 15,000 we
have oft defeated their armies of 50,000 or 60,000;
ſtands it with reaſon of war to expect the like ſucceſs
ſtill? eſpecially ſince the uſe of arms is changed, and
for the bow, proper for men of our ſtrength, the
caliver begins to be generally received."

Lord Herbert's Life and Reign of Henry VIII.
p. 18. edit. 1649.

" Becauſe alſo unlawful games kept men from
ſhooting in the long bow, they were put down,
and archery commanded. For the better under-
ſtanding

standing of which act, another past, whereby the cross bow also was forbidden."

Ibid. p. 19.

" The law of archery, made before, was not only confirmed but made perpetual: so that, notwithstanding the use of calivers or hand-guns (for musquets were not yet known) it was thought fit to continue the bow. While he that carries the caliver goes unarmed, the arrow will have the same effect within its distance as the bullet, and can for one shot return two. Besides, as they used their halberts with their bows, they could fall on the enemy with great advantage."

Ibid. p. 55.

" Greaves in his Pyramidographia says, *Some Turkish bows are of such strength as to pierce a plank six inches thick. I speak what I have seen.* And Barclay in his Icon Animorum, speaking of the Turkish bow (which differed very little in form from the long bow anciently in use among us, being drawn by the hand without the help of the rack that is used to some other bows) says, *I was an eye witness how one of these bows, with a little arrow, did pierce through a piece of steel three fingers thick.*"

Hooper's Rational Recreations, Vol. I. p. 198. edit. 1783.

[x]

In Partitiones Sagittarias ROGERI ASCHAMI, GUALTERUS HADDONUS *Cantabrigiensis* * Regius.

MITTERE qui celeres summa velit arte Sagittas,

Ars erit ex isto summa profecta libro.

Quicquid habent arcus rigidi, nervique rotundi,

Sumere si libet, hoc sumere fonte licet.

ASCHAMUS *est author, magnum quem fecit* APOLLO,

Arte sua, magnum PALLAS & *arte sua.*

Docta manus dedit hunc, dedit hunc mens docta libellum

Quæ videt ars, usus visa parata facit.

Optimus hæc author quia tradidit optima scripta.

Convenit hæc nobis optima velle sequi.

* Of King's College.

TO ALL THE

GENTLEMEN AND YOMEN

OF

ENGLANDE.

*B*IAS the wyſe man came to *Creſus* the riche
Kinge, on a time, when he was makinge newe
ſhippes, purpoſinge to have ſubdued by water the
out iſles lying betwixte *Grece* and *Aſia Minor.*
" What newes nowe in *Grece?*" ſayth the Kinge
to *Bias.* " None other newes but theſe," ſayth
Bias: " that the iſles of *Grece* have prepared a
" wonderful company of horſemen to over-run
" *Lydia* withal." " There is nothing under hea-
" ven, ſayth the Kinge, that I would ſo ſoone
" wiſh,

" wifh, as that they durft be fo bolde, to meete
" us on the land with horfe." " And thinke you,"
" fayth *Bias*, " that there is any thinge which
" they would fooner wifhe, then that you fhould
" be fo fonde, to meete them on the water with
" fhippes?" And fo *Crefus*, hearing not the true
newes, but perceyving the wyfe mannes minde and
counfell, both gave then over makinge of his fhippes,
and left alfo behinde him a wonderful example for
al common wealthes to followe: that is, evermore
to regarde and fet moft by that thinge wherunto
nature hath made them moft apt, and ufe hath
made them moft fitte.

By this matter I meane the fhooting in the longe
bow, for *Englifhemen*: which thinge, with al my
hart I do wifhe, and if I were of * authority, I
would counfell all the gentlemen and yomen of
Englande, not to chaunge it with any other thinge,
howe good foever it feeme to be, but that ftil, according to the olde wont of *Englande*, youth fhould
ufe it for the moft honeft paftime in peace, that
men might handle it as a moft fure weapon in
warre. Other † ftronge weapons, which both ex-

* Authority is here ufed not for Power, but for Credit or Influence.

† Fire-arms began about this time to be made, for the hand ordnance or
great guns feem to have been near a century employed in war before hand-
guns were much ufed.

perience

perience doth prove to be good, and the wifedome
of the Kinges Majefty and his counfel provides to
be had, are not ordayned to take awaye fhooting:
but that both, not compared together, whether
fhould be better than the other, but fo joyned together, that the one fhould be alwayes an ayde and
helpe for the other, might fo ftrengthen the realme
on all fides, that no kinde of enemye, in any kinde
of weapon, might paffe and go beyonde us.

For this purpofe I, partlye provoked by the counfell of fome gentlemen, partlye moved by the love
which I have alwayes borne toward fhootinge, have
written this litle treatife; wherein, if I have not
fatisfyed any man, I truft he will the rather be content with my doinge, becaufe I am (I fuppofe) the
firft, which hath faid any thinge in this matter,
(and fewe beginninges be perfect, fayth wyfe men:)
and alfo becaufe, if I have faide amiffe, I am content that any man amende it, or, if I have faid to
litle, any man that will to adde what him pleafeth
to it.

My minde is, in profiting and pleafing every
man, to hurt or difpleafe no man, intending none
other purpofe, but that youth might be ftirred to
c   labour,

labour, honeſt paſtime, and virtue, and as much
as laye in me, plucked from ydlenes, unthrifty
games and vice: which thinge I have laboured
onlye in this booke, ſhewinge howe fit ſhootinge
is for all kindes of men; howe honeſt a paſtime
for the minde; howe holſome an exerciſe for the
bodye; not vile for great men to uſe, not coſtly
for poore men to ſuſtayne, not lurking in holes and
corners for ill men at their pleaſure to miſuſe it, but
abydinge in the open ſighte and face of the worlde,
for good men if it fault by theyr wyſedome to
correct it.

And here I would deſire al gentlemen and yomen to uſe this paſtime in ſuch a meane, that the
outragiouſneſs of great gaminge ſhould not hurt the
honeſtye of ſhootinge, which, of his owne nature,
is always joyned with honeſtye: yet for mennes
faultes oftentimes blamed unworthelye, as all good
thinges have bene, and evermore ſhal be.

If any man would blame me, eyther for takinge
ſuch a matter in hande, or els for wrytinge it in the
Engliſhe tongue, this aunſwere I may make him,
that when the beſt of the realme thincke it honeſt
for them to uſe, I, one of the meaneſt ſorte, ought
not

not to fuppofe it vile for me to wryte : and thoughe to have written it in another tongue, had bene both more profitable for my ftudy, and alfo more * honeft for my name, yet I can thincke my laboure well beftowed, if with a little hindrance of my profite and name, may come any furtherance to the pleafure or commodity of the gentlemen and yomen of *Englande*, for whofe fake I toke this matter in hand. And as for the *Latine* or *Greeke* tongue, everye thinge is fo excellentlye done in them, that none can do better : In the *Englifhe* tongue, contrary, everye thinge in a maner fo meanlye both for the matter and handelinge, that no man can do worfe. For therein the leaft learned, for the moft part, have bene alwayes moft readye to write. And they which had leaft hope in *Latine*, have bene moft bould in *Englifhe* : when furelye everye man that is moft readye to talke, is not moft able to write. He that will write well in any tongue, muft follow this counfel of *Ariftotle*, to fpeake as the comon people do, to thinke as wyfe men do : as fo fhoulde everye man underftand him, and the judgement of wyfe men alowe him. Manye *Englifhe* writers have not done fo, but ufinge ftraunge wordes, as *Latine*, *Frenche*, and *Italian*, do make

* Honeft is here ufed for honourable.

all

all thinges darke and harde. Ones I communed with a man which reasoned the *Englishe* tongue to be enriched and encreased thereby, sayinge : " Who " will not prayse that feast where a man shall " drincke at a dinner both wyne, ale and beere ?" " Truly (quoth I) they be al good, every one " taken by himselfe alone, but if you put malvesye " and sacke, redde wyne and white, ale and beere, " and al in one pot, you shall make a drincke not " easye to be knowen, nor yet holsome for the " bodye." *Cicero*, in folowing *Isocrates*, *Plato* and *Demosthenes*, encreased the *Latine* tongue after another sort. This way, because divers men that wryte, do not know, they can neyther folow it, because of theyr ignoraunce, nor yet will prayse it for over arrogancye, two faultes, seldome the one out of the others companye. *Englishe* writers, by diversity of time, have taken dyvers matters in hand. In our fathers time no thinge was read but bookes of fayned chevalrie, wherin a man by readinge shoulde be led to none other ende, but onely to manslaughter and baudrye. If anye man suppose they were good enough to passe the time with all, he is deceived. For surely vaine wordes do worke no small thinge in vaine, ignorant, and young mindes, especially if they be geven any thinge

thereunto

thereunto of their owne nature. Thefe bookes (as
I have heard fay) were made the moft part in ab-
bayes, and monafteries, a very likely and fit fruite
of fuch an ydle and blind kind of lyving. In our
tyme now, when every man is geven to know,
much rather than to live wel, very many do write,
but after fuch a fafhion as very many do fhoote.
Some fhooters take in hande ftronger bowes, than
they be able to * maintaine. This thinge maketh
them fome time to over fhoote the marke, fome
time to fhoote far wyde, and perchaunce hurt fome
that looke on. Other that never learned to fhoote,
nor yet knoweth good fhaft nor bow, wil be as bufy
as the beft, but fuche one commonlye † plucketh
down a fide, and crafty archers which be againft
him, will be both glad of him, and alfo ever redye
to lay and bet with him: It were better for fuch
one to fit down than fhote. Other there be, which
have very good bow and fhafts, and good knowledge in fhootinge, but they have been brought up
in fuch evill favoured fhootinge, that they can
neither fhoote ‡ fayre nor yet nere. If any man
will applye thefe thinges together, fhal not fe the

* To maintaine is to manage.

† To pluck down afide, we believe, is to fhoot on one fide into the ground.

‡ Neither fhoot gracefully nor exactly.

one

one far differ from the other. And I alſo, amonges
all other, in wryting this litle treatiſe, have folowed
ſome yong ſhooters, which both wil begin to ſhote,
for a litle money, and alſo wil uſe to ſhoote ones
or twiſe about the marke for nought, afore they
begin a good. And therefore dyd I take this litle
matter in hand, to aſſay myſelfe, and hereafter, by
the grace of God, if iudgement of wyſe men, that
loke on, thinke that I can do anye good, I may
perchance caſt my ſhaft among other, for better
game. Yet in writing this booke, ſome man wil
marveile perchance, why that I beyng an unper-
fect ſhooter, ſhould take in hand to write of makyng a perfect archer : the ſame man, peradventure,
wil marveile howe a whetſtone, whiche is blunt, can
make the edge of a knife ſharpe : I would the ſame
man ſhould conſider alſo, that in going about any
matter, there be four things to be conſidered,
doing, ſaying, thinncking, and perfectneſs : Firſt,
there is no man that doth ſo well, but he can ſay
better, ‖ or els ſome men, whiche be now ſtarke
nought, ſhould be too good : Again, no man can
utter with his tongue, ſo wel as he is able to ima-

‖ This paſſage is ſomewhat confuſed. The meaning is, that if from what
men ſay we could infer what they do, we might think many to be good,
whom we hear talking well, whom yet we know to be bad, becauſe they
live ill.

gine

gine with his minde, and yet perfectnes itselfe is
far above al thinkinge. Then, seyng that saying
is one step nerer perfectnes than doing, let every
man leave marveyling why my worde shal rather expresse, than my dede shall perfourme, perfect
shootinge.

I trust no man will be offended with this litle
booke, excepte it be some fletchers and bowyers,
thinkinge hereby that many that love shootinge
shall be taught to refuse such noughtye wares as
they woulde utter. Honest * fletchers and bowyers do not so, and they that be unhonest, ought
rather to amende themselves for doing ill, than be
angrye with me for saying well. A fletcher hath
even as good a quarell to be angrye with an archer
that refuseth an ill shaft, as a blade-smith hath to
a fletcher that forsaketh to bye of him a noughtye
knyfe; for as an archer must be content that a
fletcher knowe a good shafte in every pointe for
the perfecter makyng of it; so an honest fletcher
will also be content that a shooter know a good
shafte in everye pointe, for the perfecter usinge of
it; because the one knoweth like a fletcher howe
to make it, the other knoweth like an archer how

* Fletcher is an arrow maker.

to

to use it. And seinge the knowledge is one in them both, yet the ende divers; surely that fletcher is an enemy to archers and artillery, which cannot be content that an archer knowe a shafte, as well for his use in shootinge, as he himselfe should knowe a shafte, for his advantage in sellinge. And the rather, because shaftes be not made so much to be sold, but chieflye to be used. And seinge that use and occupyinge is the ende why a shafte is made, the makyng, as it were, a meane for ocupyinge, surelye the knowledge in every point of a good shafte, is more to be required in a shooter than a fletcher.

Yet, as I sayde before, no honest fletcher will be angrye with me, seing I do not teache howe to make a shafte, which belongeth onlye to a good fletcher, but to knowe and handle a shafte, which belongeth to an archer. And this litle booke, I trust, shall please and profit both parties: for good bowes and shaftes shall be better knowen to the commodity of all shooters, and good shootinge may, perchaunce, be more occupyed to the profit of all bowyers and fletchers. And thus I praye God that all fletchers, getting their lyving truly, and all archers, usinge shootinge honestlye, and all
manner

manner of men that favour artillerye, maye live continuallye in healthe and merineſſe, obeying theyr Prince as they ſhoulde, and loving God as they oughte: to whome, for all thinges, be all honour and glorye for ever. *Amen.*

ROGER ASCHAM.

TOXOPHILUS.

THE
FIRST BOOKE
OF THE
SCHOLE OF SHOOTINGE.

PHILOLOGUS.   TOXOPHILUS.

PHILOLO-
GUS. **Y**OU studye to sore, *Toxophilus.*
Tox. I will not hurt myselfe
over much, I warrant you. PHI. Take heede
you do not, for we physitions saye, that it is neyther good for the eyes in so cleare a sunne, nor yet
holesome for the body, so soone after meate, to
looke upon a mans booke. Tox. In eatinge
and studyinge I will never folowe any physicke,
for if I did, I am sure I should have small pleasure
in the one, and lesse courage in the other. But
what news drave you hither, I pray you. PHI.
Small news, trulye, but that as I came on walkinge, I fortuned to come with three or four that
went to shoote at the prickes : and when I sawe

B   not

not you amonges them, but at the laſt eſpyed you lookinge on your booke here ſo * ſadlye, I thought to come and hold you with ſome communication, leſt your booke ſhoulde run away with you. For methought by your waveringe pace, and earneſt lookinge, your booke ledde you, not you it.   Tox. Indeede, as it chaunced, my minde went faſter then my feete, for I happened here to reade in *Phedro Platonis*, a place that entreates wonderfullye of the nature of ſoules, which place, whethir it were for the paſſinge eloquence of *Plato*, and the *Greeke* tongue ; or for the highe and godlye deſcription of the matter, kepte my minde ſo occupied, that it had no leiſure to looke to my feete. For I was readynge how ſome ſoules, beinge well feathered, flewe alwayes about heaven and heavenly matters ; other ſome havinge their feathers mouted away and droupinge, ſancke downe into earthlye thinges.   PHI. I remember the place very well, and it is wonderfullye ſayd of *Plato*, and now I ſee it was no marveile thoughe your feete fayled you, ſeinge your minde flewe ſo faſte.   Tox. I am glad now that you letted me, for my heade akes with lookinge on it, and becauſe you tell me ſo, I am very ſorye that I was

* Seriouſly.

not

not with thofe good fellowes you fpake upon, for it is a very fayre day for a man to fhoote in. PHI. And methincke, you were a great deale better occupyed, and in better company, for it is a very fayre day for a man to go to his booke in. TOX. All dayes and wethers will ferve for that purpofe, and furely this occafion was ill loft. PHI. Yea, but cleare wether maketh cleare mindes, and it is beft, as I fuppofe, to fpende the beft time upon the beft thinges : and me thought you fhotte verye well, and at that marke, at whiche everye good fcholer fhoulde moft bufilye fhote at. And I fuppofe it be a great deale more pleafure alfo to fee a foule flye in *Plato*, than a fhafte flye at the prickes. I graunte you, fhootinge is not the worfte thinge in the world, yet if we fhote, and time fhote, we are not like to be great winners at the lengthe. And you know alfo we fcholers have more earneft and weightye matters in hande, nor we be not borne to paftime and playe, as you knowe well enoughe who fayeth. [1] TOX. Yet the fame man, in the fame place, *Philologe*, by your leave, doth admitte holefome, honeft, and manerlye paftimes, to be as neceffarye to be mingled with fadde matters of the minde, as eatinge and fleapinge is

[1] M. Cic. in Off.

for

for the healthe of the bodye, and yet we be borne for neyther of both. [2] And *Ariſtotle* himſelfe ſayth, that althoughe it were a fonde and a child-iſhe thinge to be to earneſt in paſtime and playe, yet doth he affirme, by the authority of the olde poet *Epicharmus*, that a man may uſe playe for earneſt matters ſake. [3] And in another place, that, as reſt is for laboure, and medecines for healthe, ſo is paſtime, at times, for ſadde and weightye ſtudye. PHI. How muche in this matter is to be geven to the authoritye eyther of *Ariſtotle* or *Tullye* I can not tell, ſeinge ſadde men may well enoughe ſpeake merilye for a merye mat-ter: this I am ſure, whiche thinge this fayre wheate (God ſave it) maketh mee remember, that thoſe huſbandmen whiche ryſe earlyeſt, and come lateſt home, and are contente to have theyr dinner and other drinkynges broughte into the fielde to them, for feare of looſinge of tyme, have fatter barnes in the harveſt, than they which will eyther ſleape at noone tyme of the day, or els make merye with theyr neighbours at the ale. And ſo a ſcholer that purpoſeth to be a good huſbande, and deſyr-eth to reape and enioye much fruite of learninge,

[2] Ariſt. de moribus, 10. 6.   [3] Ariſt. Pol. 8. 3.

muſt

muſt till and ſowe * thereafter. Our beſt ſeede
tyme, whiche be ſcholers, as it is very tymely,
and when we be yonge: ſo it endureth not over
long, and therefore it may not be let ſlippe one
houre: our grounde is very harde, and full of
weedes, our horſe wherewith we be drawen very
wilde, as *Plato* ſayth. 4 And infinite other mo
lettes, which will make a thriftye ſcholer take
heede howe he ſpendeth his time in ſport and playe.
Tox. That *Ariſtotle* and *Tullye* ſpake earneſtlye,
and as they thoughte, the earneſte matter whiche
they entreate upon, doth plainlye prove. And, as
for your huſbandrye, it was more † probablye
tolde with apte wordes proper to the thinge, than
thoroughlye proved with reaſons belonginge to our
matter. For, contrarywyſe, I heard myſelfe a good
huſbande at his booke once ſaye, that to omitte
ſtudye ſome tyme of the daye, and ſome tyme of
the yeare, made as much for the encreaſe of learnynge, as to let the lande lye ſome tyme falloe,
maketh for the better increaſe of corne. This we
ſee, if the lande be plowed every yeare, the corne
cometh thinne up: the ear is ſhort, the grain is
ſmall, and, when it is brought into the barne and

4 In Phædro.

* In order to it.　　　　† Probably is ſpeciouſly.

threſhed,

threſhed, geveth very evill ‡ faule. So thoſe which never leave poringe on theyr bookes, have oftentimes as thinne invention, as other poore men have, and as ſmall witte and weight in it as in other mens. And thus your huſbandrye, methincke, is more like the life of a covetous ſnudge that ofte very evill proves, then the labour of a good huſbande that knoweth well what he doth. And ſurelye the beſt wittes to learninge muſt needes have much recreation and ceaſynge from theyr booke, or els they marre themſelves; when baſe and dompiſhe wittes can never be hurte with continual ſtudye, as ye ſee in lutinge, that a treble minikin ſtringe muſt alwayes be let downe, but at ſuch tyme as when a man muſt needes playe, when the baſe and dull ſtringe needeth never to be moved out of his place. The ſame reaſon I finde true in two bowes that I have, whereof the one is quicke of caſte ‖ tricke, and trimme both for pleaſure and profite: the other is a lugge ſlowe of caſte, followinge the ſtringe, more ſure for to laſt, then pleaſant for to uſe. Now, Sir, it chaunced this other night, one in my chamber would needes bende them to prove their ſtrengthe, but (I cannot tell howe) they were both lefte bente till the

‡ Faule or Fall, is Produce.   ‖ Tricke or Trickſy, is neat, nice, elegant.

next

next day after dinner : and when I came to them, purpofinge to have gone on fhootinge, I founde my good bowe clene * caft on the one fyde, and as weake as water, that furelye, if I were a riche man, I had rather have fpent a crowne : and as for my lugge, it was not one whit the worfe, but fhotte by and by as well and as farre as ever it did. And even fo, I am fure that good wittes, excepte they be let downe lyke a treble ftringe, and un-bente lyke a good cafting bowe, they will never laft and be able to continue in ftudye. And I know where I fpake this, *Philologe*, for I would not fay thus much afore younge men, for they will take foone occafion to ftudye litle ynoughe. But I faye it therefore, becaufe I knowe, as litle ftudye getteth litle learnyng, or none at all, fo the moft ftudye getteth not the moft learninge of all. For a mans witte fore occupied in earneft ftudye muft be as well recreated with fome honeft paftime, as the bodye fore laboured mufte be refrefhed with fleape and quietneffe, or elfe it cannot endure verye longe, as the noble poete fayth :

† What thinge wants quiet and mery reft, endures but a fmall while. **Ovid.**

* Caft is warped. The word is ftill ufed by artificers.

† If this line was fo tranflated when this treatife was firft written in 1544, it is the oldeft Englifh hexameter that we remember.

And

And I promife you fhootinge, by my iudgement, is the moft honefte paftime of all, and fuche one, I am fure, of all other, that hindereth learninge litle or nothinge at all, whatfoever you and fome other faye, which are a great deale forer againft it alwayes than you neede to be. PHI. Hindereth learninge litle or nothinge at all! that were a marveile to me trulye, and I am fure, feinge you fay fo, you have fome reafon wherwith you can defende fhootinge with all, and as for will, (for the love that you beare towarde fhootinge) I thincke there fhall lacke none in you. Therfore, feinge we have fo good leyfure both, and no bodye by to trouble us: and you fo willinge and able to defende it, and I fo readye and glade to heare what may be faid of it, I fuppofe we cannot paffe the time better over, neyther you for the ‡ honeftye of your fhootinge, nor I for mine own minde fake, than to fee what can be fayed with it, or againft it, and fpecialye in thefe days, when fo many doth ufe it, and every man, in a manner, doth commune of it. TOX. To fpeake of fhootinge, *Philologe*, trulye I would I were fo able, eyther as I myfelfe am willinge, or yet as the matter deferveth; but feinge with wifhinge we cannot have one nowe worthy, which fo worthye a thinge

‡ Honefty is Honour.

can

can worthelye prayſe, and although I had rather have any other to do it than myſelfe, yet myſelfe rather then no other, I will not fayle to ſay in it what I can. Wherein if I ſay litle, laye that of my litle habilitye, not of the matter itſelfe, which deſerveth no litle thinge to be ſayde of it. PHI. If it deſerve no litle thinge to be ſayde of it, *Toxophile*, I marveile how it chaunceth than, that no man hitherto hath written anye thinge of it: wherein you muſte graunt me, that eyther the matter is nought, unworthye, and barren to be written upon, or els ſome men are to blame, which both love it and uſe it, and yet coulde never finde in theyr harte, to ſaye one good woorde of it, ſeinge that verye triflinge matters hath not lacked great learned men to ſet them oute, as * gnattes and nuttes, and many other more like thinges, wherefore eyther you may honeſtlye laye very great faulte upon men, becauſe they never yet prayſed it, or els I may iuſtlye take away no litle thinge from ſhootinge, becauſe it never yet deſerved it. TOX. Truelye, herein, *Philologe*, you take not ſo much from it, as you geve to it. For great and commodious thynges are never greatlye prayſed, not becauſe they be not worthye, but becauſe theyr excellencye

---

* The Gnat of Virgil, and the Nut of Ovid.

C

needeth

needeth no man his prayſe, havinge all theyr commendation of themſelfe, not borrowed of other
men his lippes, which rather prayſe themſelfe, in
ſpeakinge muche of a litle thinge, then that matter
which they entreat upon. Great and good thinges
be not prayſed : " For who ever prayſed *Hercu-*
" *les* ?" (ſayth the *Greeke* proverbe.) And that
no man hitherto hath written anye booke of ſhootinge, the faulte is not to be layed in the thinge
which was worthye to be written upon, but of
men which were negligente in doinge it, and this
was the cauſe thereof as I ſuppoſe. Menne that
uſed ſhootinge moſt and knewe it beſt, were not
learned : men that were learned, uſed litle ſhootinge, and were ignoraunt in the nature of the thinge,
and ſo fewe men have bene that hitherto were able
to write upon it. Yet how long ſhootinge hath
continued, what common wealthes hath moſt uſed
it, how honeſt a thinge it is for all men, what
kinde of lyvinge ſoever they folowe, what pleaſure
and profite commeth of it, both in peace and warre,
all maner of tongues and writers, *Hebrewe*, *Greeke*,
and *Latine*, hath ſo plentifullye ſpoken of it, as of
few other thinges like. So what ſhootinge is,
howe many kindes there is of it, what goodneſſe
is ioyned with it, is tolde : onlye how it is to be
learned

learned and broughte to a perfectnesse amonges men, is not tolde. PHI. Then, *Toxophile*, if it be so as you do saye, let us go forwarde, and examine howe plentifullye this is done that you speake; and, first, of the invention of it, then what honestye and profite is in the use of it, both for warre and peace, more than in other pastimes; last of all howe it oughte to be learned amonges men, for the encrease of it. Which thinge if you do, not onlye I nowe, for your communication, but many other mo, when they shall knowe of it, for your labour, and shootinge itselfe also (if it could speake) for your kindnesse, will con you very muche thancke. TOX. What goode thinges men speake of shootinge, and what good thinges shootinge bringes to men, as my witte and knowledge will serve me,. gladly shall I saye my minde. But howe the thinge is to be learned, I will surelye leave to some other, which, both for greater experience in it, and also for their learnynge, can set it out better than I. PHI. Well, as for that, I knowe both what you can do in shootinge, by experience, and that you can also speake well ynough of shootinge, for your learnynge: but go on with the first part. And I do not doubt, but what my desire, what your love towardes it, the

honeſtye of ſhootinge, the profit that may come
thereby to many others, ſhall get the ſecond part
out of you at the laſt.   Tox. Of the firſt find-
ers out of ſhootinge, divers men diverſlye do wryte.
5 *Claudiane* the poete ſayth, that nature geve example of ſhootinge firſt, by the * *Porpentine*, which
ſhoote his prickes, and will hitte anye thinge that
fightes with it : wherebye men learned afterwarde
did imitate the ſame, in findinge out both bowe
and ſhaftes. 6 *Plinie* referreth it to *Schythes* the
ſonne of *Jupiter*. 7 Better, and more noble wryters, brynge ſhootinge from a more noble inventour :
as *Plato*, *Calimachus*, and *Galen*, from *Apollo*. 8
Yet longe afore thoſe days we do read in the Bible
of ſhootinge expreſslye ; and alſo, if we ſhall believe 9 *Nicholas de Lyra*, *Lamech* killed *Cain* with a
ſhafte. So this great continuance of ſhootinge
dothe not a litle prayſe ſhootinge : nor that neyther dothe not a litle ſet it out, that it is referred
to the invention of *Apollo*, for the which pointe
ſhootinge is highlye prayſed of 10 *Galen :* where he
ſayth, that meane craftes be firſt founde out by men

5 C. Claudianus in Hiſtri. 6 Plin. 7. 56. 7 In Sym-
po. in hymn. ad Apoll. 8 Geneſis 21. 9 Ni. de Lyra.
10 Galenus in exhor. ad bonas artes.

* Porcupine.

or

or beaftes, as weavinge by a fpider, and fuch other:
but high and commendable fciences by Goddes, as
fhootinge and muficke by *Apollo*.   And thus fhootinge, for the neceffitye of it, ufed in *Adams* days,
for the nobleneffe of it referred to *Apollo*, hath not
bene onlye commended in all tongues and wryters,
but alfo had in great price, both in the beft common wealthes, in warre time, for the defence of
their countrye, and of all degrees of men in peace
time, both for the honeftye that is ioyned with it,
and the profite that followeth it.   PHI. Well,
as concerninge the findinge out of it, litle prayfe
is gotten to fhootinge therebye, feynge good wittes
maye moft eafilye of all finde out a triflinge matter.   But whereas you faye, that moft common
wealthes have ufed it in warre tyme, and all degrees of men may verye honeftlye ufe it in peace
tyme : I thincke you can neyther fhew by authoritye, nor yet prove by reafon.   TOX. The ufe
of it in warre tyme, I will declare hereafter.   And
firft, howe all kindes and fortes of men (what degree foever they be) hath at all tymes afore, and
nowe may honeftlye ufe it, the example of moft
noble men very well doth prove.

Cyaxares

[1] *Cyaxares* the Kinge of the *Medees*, and great grand father to *Cyrus*, kept a fort of *Sythians* with him onlye for this purpofe, to teache his fonne *Aftyages* to fhoote. [2] *Cyrus*, beinge a childe, was broughte uppe in fhootinge; which thinge *Zenophon* would never have made mention on, excepte it had bene fitte for all Princes to have ufed; feinge that *Zenophon* wrote *Cyrus* lyfe, [3] (as *Tullye* fayth) not to fhew what *Cyrus* did, but what all maner of Princes, both in paftymes and earneft matters, ought to do.

Darius, the firft of that name, and kinge of *Perfia*, fhewed plainlye howe fitte it is for a Kinge to love and ufe fhootinge, which commaunded this fentence to be graven in his tombe, for a princelye memorye and prayfe.

> Darius the Kinge lyeth buried here,
> That in fhootinge and rydinge had never pere.   Strabo 15.

Agayne, [4] *Domitian* the Emperour was fo cunninge in fhootinge, that he coulde fhote betwixt a mans fingers ftanding afarre off, and never hurte him. *Commodus* alfo was fo excellente, and had

---

[1] Herod. in Clio. [2] Xen. in Infti. Cyri. 1.   Ad Quint. Fra. 1. 1. [4] Suet.

so sure a hand in it, that there was nothinge within his reach and shote, but he would hit in what place he would ; as beasts runninge, eyther in the head, or in the harte, and never misse ; as [5] *Herodiane* sayeth he sawe himselfe, or els he could never have believed it.   PHI. Indeede you prayse shootinge very well, in that you shew that *Domitian* and *Commodus* love shootinge, such an ungratious couple, I am sure, as a man shall not finde agayne, if he raked all hell for them.   TOX. Well, even as I will not commend theyr ilnesse, so oughte not you to disprayse theyr goodnesse ; and indeede, the iudgmente of *Herodian* uppon *Commodus* is true of them bothe, and that was this : that besyde strengthe of bodye and good shootinge, they had no princelye thinge in them ; whiche sayinge, methincke, commendes shootinge wonderfullye, calling it a princelye thinge.   Forthermore, howe commendable shootinge is for Princes : [6] *Themistius*, the noble philosopher, shewethe in a certaine oration made to *Theodosius* the Emperour, wherein he dothe commende him for three thinges, that he used of a childe : For shootinge, for ryding of an horse well, and for feates of armes.

[5] Herodia 1.   [6] Themist. in Orat. 6.

Moreover,

Moreover, not onely Kinges and Emperours have been broughte up in fhootinge, but alfo the beft common wealthes that ever were, have made goodlye acts and lawes for it, as the [7] *Perfians,* whiche under *Cyrus* conquered, in a maner, all the world, had a lawe that their children fhoulde learne three thinges onlye from five yeares oulde unto twenty, to ryde an horfe well, to fhoote well, to fpeake truthe alwayes and never lye. The *Romaynes* [8] (as *Leo* the Emperour in his book of fleightes of warre telleth) had a lawe that everye man fhoulde ufe fhootinge in peace tyme, while he was forty yeare oulde, and that everye houfe fhoulde have a bowe, and forty fhaftes, ready for all needes ; the omittinge of which lawe (fayth *Leo*) amonge the youthe, hathe bene the onlye occafion why the *Romaynes* loft a great deale of theyr empyre. But more of this I will fpeake when I come to the profite of fhootinge in warre. If I fhoulde rehearfe the ftatutes made of noble Princes of *Englande* in parliamentes, for the fettinge forwarde of fhootinge, throughe this realme, and fpecially that acte made for fhootinge the thirde yeare of the raigne of our moft dreade Soveraigne Lord Kinge

---

[7] Herod. in Clio.   [8] Leo de ftratag. 20.

Henrye

Henrye the VIII. I coulde be verye longe. But thefe fewe examples, fpeciallye of fo greate men and noble common wealthes, fhall ftande in fteede of manye.   PHI. That fuche Princes, and fuche common wealthes have muche regarded fhootinge, you have well declared. But whye fhootinge oughte fo of itfelfe to be regarded, you have fcarcelye yet proved.

TOX. Examples, I graunt, out of hiftoryes do fhewe a thinge to be fo, not prove a thinge why it fhould be fo. Yet this I fuppofe, that neyther great mens qualityes, beinge commendable, be withoute great auctoritye, for other men honeftlye to followe them; nor yet thofe great learned men that wrote fuch thinges, lacke good reafon iuftlye at all tymes for anye other to approve them. Princes, beinge children, oughte to be brought uppe in fhootinge, bothe becaufe it is an exercife moft holfome, and alfo a paftime mofte honeft : wherein laboure prepareth the bodye to hardneffe, the minde to couragioufneffe, fufferinge neyther the one to be marde with tenderneffe, nor yet the other to be hurte with ydleneffe, as we reade howe *Sardanapalus* and fuch other were, becaufe they were not brought up with outwarde honeft painfull

D   paftimes

paſtimes to be men, but cockerde up with inwarde noughtye ydle wantonneſſe to be women. For howe fitte laboure is for all youthe, *Jupiter* or els *Minos* amonges them of *Greece*, and *Lycurgus* amonge the *Lacedemonians*, 9 do ſhewe by theyr lawes, whiche never ordeyned anye thinge for the bringinge up of youth, that was not ioyned with labour ; and that labour whiche is in ſhootinge of all other is beſt, both becauſe it encreaſeth ſtrengthe, and preſerveth healthe moſt, beinge not vehement, but moderate, not overlayinge anye one parte with wearineſſe, but ſoftlye exerciſinge everye parte with equalneſſe, as the arms and breaſtes with drawinge, the other parts with goinge, beinge not ſo painfull for the labour, as pleaſaunt for the paſtime, 10 which exerciſe, by the iudgment of the beſte phyſitions, is moſt alowable. By ſhootinge alſo is the minde honeſtlye exerciſed, where a man alwayes deſireth to be beſt, (which is a word of honeſtye) and that by the ſame way, that vertue itſelfe dothe, coveting to come nigheſt a more perfitte ende, or mean ſtandinge betwixte two extreames, eſchewinge ſhorte, or gone, or eyther ſyde wyde, for the which cauſes *Ariſtotle* himſelfe ſayth, that 1 ſhootinge and

9 Cic. 2. Tuſ. Qu. 10 Galen. 2. de Santuend. 1 Ariſ-
tot. de morib.

vertue

vertue be very lyke. Moreover, that shootinge of all other is the most honest pastyme, and that leaste occasion to naughtinesse is ioyned with it, two thinges verye plainly do prove, whiche be, as a man would saye, the tutors and overseers to shootinge : daye light, and open place where everye man dothe come, the mainteiners and keepers of shootinge, from all unhoneste doinge. If shootinge fault at anye time, it hydes it not, it lurkes not in corners and huddermother : but openlye accuseth and bewrayeth itselfe, which is the next way to amendment, as wyse men do saye. And these thinges, I suppose, be sighes, not of naughtinesse, for anye man to disalowe it, but rather verye plaine tokens of honestye, for every man to prayse it. The use of shootinge also in great mennes children shall greatly encrease the love and use of shootinge in all the residue of youth. For meane mennes mindes love to be like great men, as [2] *Plato* and *Isocrates* do saye. And that everye bodye shoulde learne to shoote, when they be younge, defence of the common wealthe doth require when they be oulde, whiche thinge cannot be done mightelye when they be men, excepte

[2] In Nic.

D 2

they

they learne it perfetlye when they be boyes. And therefore ſhootinge of all paſtymes is moſt fitte to be uſed in childhoode : becauſe it is an imitation of moſt earneſte thinges to be done in manhode. Wherefore, ſhootinge is fitte for great mennes children, both becauſe it ſtrengtheneth the bodye with holſome laboure, and pleaſeth the minde with honeſt paſtyme, and alſo encourageth all other youthe earneſtlye to followe the ſame. And theſe reaſons (as I ſuppoſe) ſtirred uppe both great men to bringe uppe their children in ſhootinge, and alſo noble common wealthes ſo ſtraitly to commaunde ſhootinge. Therefore ſeinge Princes, moved by honeſt occaſions, have in all common wealthes uſed ſhootinge, I ſuppoſe there is no other degree of men, neyther lowe nor hye, learned nor leude, younge nor olde. * PHI. You ſhall neede wade no further in this matter, *Toxophile,* but if you can prove me that ſcholers and men geven to learnynge maye honeſtlye uſe ſhootinge, I will ſoon graunt you that all other ſortes of men may not onlye lawfullye, but oughte of dutye to uſe it. But I thincke you cannot prove but that all theſe examples of ſhootinge broughte from ſo long a tyme, uſed of ſo noble Princes, confirmed

* Here ſeems to be ſome deficiency in the copy.

by

by fo wyfe mennes lawes and iudgements, are fet
afore temporal men, onelye to followe them ;
whereby they maye the better and ftronglyer defende the common wealth withall ; and nothinge
belongeth to fcholars and learned men, which have
another part of the common wealthe, quiete and
peaceable put to theyr cure and charge, whofe
ende, as it is diverfe from the other, fo there is
no one way that leadeth to them bothe   Tox.
I graunt, *Philologe*, that fcholers and layemen have
divers offices and charges in the common wealthe,
which requires divers bringyng uppe in theyr youthe,
if they fhall do them as they oughte to do in theyr
age.   Yet as temporal men of neceffitye are compelled to take fomewhat of learnynge to do theyr
office the better withall, fo fcholars may the boldlyer borrowe fomewhat of layemennes paftymes to
mainteine theyr healthe in ftudye withal.   And
furelye, of all other thynges, fhootinge is neceffarye for bothe fortes to learne.   Which thinge,
when it has bene evermore ufed in *Englande*, howe
much good it hath done, both old men and chronicles do tell : and alfo our enemies can bear us
recorde.   For if it be true as I have heard faye,
when the Kinge of *Englande* hath bene in *Fraunce*,
the Prieftes at home, becaufe they were archers,
                                               have

have bene able to overthrow all *Scotlande*. Againe, there is another thynge, which above all other dothe move me, not onlye to love fhootinge, to prayfe fhootinge, to exhorte all other to fhootinge, but alfo to ufe fhootinge myfelfe: and that is our late Kinge *Henrye* the eyghte his moft royal purpofe and will, whiche in all his ftatutes generallye dothe commaund men, and with his owne mouth moft gently did exhorte men, and by his great giftes and rewardes greatlye did encourage men, and with his moft princelye example verye often did provoke all other men to the fame. But here you will come with temporall man and fcholer. I tell you plainly, fcholer or unfcholer, yea if I were twenty fcholers, I woulde thincke it were mye dutye, bothe with exhortinge men to fhoote, and alfo with fhootinge myfelfe, to helpe to fet forwarde that thinge which the Kinge his wyfedome, and his counfaile, fo greatlye laboure to have go forward : which thinge furelye they did, becaufe they knew it to be, in warre, the defence and wall of our countreye ; in peace, an exercife moft holfome for the bodye, a paftyme moft honefte for the minde, and, as I am able to prove myfelfe, of all other mofte fitte and agreeable with learnynge and learned men.   PHI. If you can prove this
thynge

thynge fo plainlye, as you fpeak it earneftlye, then will I not onelye thincke as you do, but become a fhooter, and do as you do. But yet beware, I fay, left you, for the great love you beare towarde fhootinge, blindly iudge of fhootinge. For love, and all other too earneft affections, be not for noughte painted blinde. Take heede (I fay) left you prefer fhootinge afore other paftymes, as one *Balbinus*, through blinde affection, preferred his lover before all other women, although fhe was deformed with a *Polyppus* in her nofe. And although fhootinge may be meete fome tyme for fome fcholers, and fo forth; yet the fitteft alwayes is to be preferred. Therefore, if you will needes graunt fcholers paftyme and recreation of theyr mindes, let them ufe (as manye of them do) *Muficke* and playinge on inftruments, thinckinge moft feemlye for all fcholers, and moft regarded alwayes of *Apollo* and the *Mufes*. Tox. Even as I cannot denye but fome *Muficke* is fit for learninge, fo I truft you cannot choofe but graunt, that fhootinge is fit alfo, as [3] *Callimachus* doth fignifye in this verfe:

---Both merie fonges and good fhootinge delighteth Apollo.---

[3] Cal. hym.

But

But as concerninge whether of them is moſt fitte for learninge, and ſcholers to uſe, you may ſaye what you will for your pleaſure, this I am ſure that *Plato* and *Ariſtotle* bothe, in theyr bookes entreatinge of the common wealthe, where they ſhewe howe youthe ſhould be brought uppe in four thinges, in readinge, in writinge, in exerciſe of bodye, and ſinginge, do make mention of *Muſicke* and all kyndes of it, wherein they bothe agree, that *Muſicke* uſed amonges the *Lydians* is very ill for young men, which be ſtudentes for vertue and learnynge, for a certaine nyce, ſofte, and ſmoothe ſweteneſſe of it, whiche would rather entice them to noughtines, then ſtirre them to honeſtye.

An other kinde of *Muſicke*, invented by the *Dorians*, they bothe wonderfully prayſe, alowinge it to be very fitte for the ſtudye of vertue and learninge, becauſe of a manlye, roughe and ſtoute ſounde in it, whiche ſhould encourage younge ſtomakes to attempte manlye matters. Nowe whether theſe balades and roundes, theſe galiardes, pavanes and daunces, ſo nycelye fingered, ſo ſweetlye tuned, be lyker the *Muſicke* of the *Lydians*, or the *Dorians*, you that be learned iudge. And whatſoever ye iudge, this I am ſure, that lutes, harpes, all maner

maner of pypes, barbitons, fambukes, with other
inftrumentes every one, whiche ftandeth by fine
and quicke fingeringe, be condemned of *Ariftotle*,
as not to be broughte in and ufed among them,
which ftudye for learnynge and vertue.

Pallas, when fhe had invented a pipe, cafte it
awaye, not fo muche, fayth ⁴ *Ariftotle*, becaufe it
deformed her face, but muche rather becaufe fuch
an inftrument belonged nothinge to learninge.
Howe fuche inftrumentes agree with learninge, the
goodlye agreement betwixt *Apollo* God of learninge, and *Marfias* the *Satyr*, defender of pypinge,
dothe well declare, where *Marfias* had his fkinne
quite pulled over his heade for his laboure.

Muche *Muficke* marreth mennes maners, fayth
Galen, althoughe fome men will faye that it dothe
not fo, but rather recreateth and maketh quicke a
mannes minde, yet methincke, by reafon it doth
as honye dothe to mannes ftomacke, which at firft
receiveth it well, but afterward it maketh it unfit
to abyde any good ftronge nourifhinge meate, or
els any holfome fharpe and quicke drincke. And
even fo in a maner thefe inftrumentes make a mans

⁴ Arift. Pol.

E

wittes

wittes so softe a smothe, so tender and quaisye,
that they be lesse able to broke stronge and toughe
studye. Wittes be not sharpened, but rather dul-
led and made blunt, with suche sweete softnesse,
even as good edges be blonter, whiche men whette
uppon soft chalke stones.

And these thinges to be true, not onlye *Plato*,
Aristotle, and *Galen*, prove by authoritye of reason, but also ⁵ *Herodotus* and other writers, shewe
by plaine and evident example; as that of *Cyrus*,
which, after he had overcome the *Lydians*, and
taken their king *Cresus* prisoner, yet after, by the
meanes of one *Pactyas*, a very heady man amonges
the *Lydians*, they rebelled againft *Cyrus* againe;
then *Cyrus* had by and by brought them to utter
destruction, if *Cresus*, beinge in good favour with
Cyrus, had not heartelye desyred him not to revenge
Pactyas faulte, in sheddinge their bloode. But if
he would folowe his counsaile, he might bringe to
passe, that theye shoulde never more rebel againft
him. And that was this, to make them weare
long kyrtils to the foote, like women, and that
everye one of them shoulde have a harpe or à lute,
and learne to playe and singe. Which thinge if

⁵ Herod. in Clio.

you

you do, fayth *Crefus*, (as he did indeed) you fhall
fee them quickly of men made women. And thus
lutinge and finginge take awaye a manlye ftomacke,
whiche fhoulde enter and pearce deepe and harde
ftudye.

Even fuch another ftorye dothe [6] *Nymphodorus*,
an olde *Greeke* hiftoriographer, write of one *Sefoftris* King of *Egypt*, which ftorye, becaufe it is
fomewhat longe, and very like in all pointes to the
other, and alfo you do well enoughe to remember
it, feinge you redde it fo late in [7] *Sophocles Com-
mentaries*, I will now paffe over. Therefore eyther
Ariftotle and *Plato* knowe not what was good and
evill for learninge and vertue, and the example of
wyfe hiftoryes be vainly fet afore us, or els the
minftrelfye of lutes, pypes, harpes, and all other
that ftandeth by fuch nyce, fine minikin fingeringe,
(fuche as the mofte parte of fcholers whom I knowe
ufe, if they ufe anye) is farre more fitte for the wo-
mannifhnes of it to dwel in the Courte among la-
dyes, than for any great thinge in it, which fhoulde
helpe good and fadde ftudye, to abide in the *Uni-
verfity* amonge fcholers But perhaps you know
fome great goodneffe of fuche *Muficke* and fuche

[6] Nymphod. [7] Comment. in Antig.

inftrumentes,

inſtrumentes, whereunto *Plato* and *Ariſtotle* his brayne coulde never attayne, and therefore I will ſaye no more againſt it.

PHI. Well, *Toxophile*, is it not enough for you to rayle uppon *Muſicke*, excepte you mocke me to? but to ſay the truthe, I never thoughte myſelfe theſe kyndes of *Muſicke* fitte for learninge, but that whiche I ſayde was rather to prove you, than to defend the matter. But yet as I woulde have this ſorte of *Muſicke* decaye among ſcholers, even ſo do I wiſhe from the bottom of my hart, that the laudable cuſtome of *Englande* to teache children their plaine ſonge and pricke ſonge, were not ſo decayed throughoute all the realme as it is. Whiche thinge how profitable it was for all ſortes of men, thoſe knewe not ſo well than which had it moſte, as they do nowe which lacke it moſt. And therefore it is true that *Teucer* ſayth in *Sophocles :*

* Seldome at all good thinges be knowen how good to be
  Before a man ſuch thinges do miſſe out of his handes. Sophocles in Aicc.

That milke is no fitter nor more naturall for the bringinge up of children than *Muſicke* is, both *Galen* proveth by auctoritye, and daily uſe teacheth by experience. For even the little babes lackinge

* Theſe lines are written in imitation of the Senarius.

the

the uſe of reaſon, are ſcarce ſo well ſtilled in ſuck-
ing their mothers pappe, as in hearinge their mother ſinge : Again, how fit youth is made, by
learninge to ſinge, for *Grammar* and other ſciences,
both we dailye do ſee, and *Plutarch* learnedly doth
prove, and *Plato* wyſelye did allow, which received
no ſcholer into his ſchole, that had not learned his
ſong before. The godlye uſe of prayſinge God,
by ſinginge in the churche, needeth not my prayſe,
ſeinge it is ſo prayſed throughe all the Scripture,
therefore now I will ſpeak nothing of it, rather
than I ſhoulde ſpeake to little of it.

Beſyde all theſe commodities, truelye two degrees of men, which have the higheſt offices under
the Kinge in all this realme, ſhall greatly lacke the
uſe of ſinginge, *Preachers* and *Lawyers*, becauſe
they ſhall not, without this, be able to rule their
breaſtes for everye purpoſe. For where is no diſ-
tinction in tellinge glade thinges and fearful thinges,
gentlenes and cruelnes, ſoftnes and vehementnes,
and ſuch like matters, there can be no great per-
ſwaſion. For the hearers, as *Tullie* ſayth, be much
affectioned, as he is that ſpeaketh. At his words
be they drawen ; if he ſtand ſtill in one faſhion,
their mindes ſtande ſtill with him : if he thunder,
they

they quake: if he chide, they fere: if he com-
plaine, they forye with him: and finallye, where
a matter is fpoken with an apte voice for everye affection, the hearers, for the moft part, are moved
as the fpeaker woulde. But when a man is alwaye
in one tune, like an humble bee, or els now in the
top of the churche, now downe that no man knowe-
eth where to have him: or piping like a reede, or
roaringe like a bull, as fome lawyers do, which
thincke they do beft, when they crye lowdeft, thefe
fhall never greatly move, as I have knowen manye
well learned have done, becaufe theyr voyce was
not ftayed afore, with learninge to finge. For all
voyces, great and fmall, bafe and fhrill, weake or
foft, may be holpen and brought to a good point
by learning to finge.

Whether this be true or not, they that ftand
moft in nede can tell befte, whereof fome I have
knowen, which, becaufe they learned not to finge,
when they were boyes, were fayne to take paine in
it, when they were men. If anye man fhoulde
heare me, *Toxophile*, that woulde thincke I did but
fondlye to fuppofe that a voyce were fo neceffarye
to be loked upon, I would afke him if he thoughte
nature a foole, for makinge fuch goodlye inftrumentes

mentes in a man, for well uttering his wordes, or els if the two noble orators *Demoſthenes* and *Cicero*, were not fooles, whereof the one did not onlye learne to ſinge of a man, but alſo was not aſhamed to learne how he ſhoulde utter his ſoundes aptlye of a dogge; the other ſetteth oute no point of *Rhetoricke* ſo fullye in all his bookes, as howe a man ſhould order his voyce for all kinde of matters.

Therefore ſeinge men, by ſpeakinge, differ and be better than beaſtes, by ſpeakinge well better than other men, and that ſinginge is an helpe towarde the ſame, as daylye experience doth teache, example of wyſe men doth alowe, authority of learned men doth approve, wherewith the foundation of youth in all good common wealthes alwayes hath bene tempered : ſurely if I were one of the parliament-houſe, I woulde not fayle to put up a bill for the amendmente of this thinge; but becauſe I am like to be none this yeare, I will ſpeake no more of it at this time.   Tox. It were pitye truly, *Philologe*, that the thinge ſhoulde be neglected, but I truſt it is not as you ſay.   Phi. The thinge is to true, for of them that come dailye to the *Univerſitye*, where one hath learned to ſingè, ſix hath not.

But

But now to our ſhootinge, *Toxophile*, againe, wherein I ſuppoſe you cannot ſay ſo much for ſhootinge to be fitte for learninge, as you have ſpoken againſt *Muſicke* for the ſame. Therefore as concerninge *Muſicke*, I can be contente to graunt you your minde : but as for ſhootinge, ſurelye I ſuppoſe that you cannot perſwade me, by no meanes, that a man can be earneſt in it, and earneſt at his booke to ; but rather I thincke that a man with a bowe on his backe, and ſhaftes under his girdle, is more fitte to wayte upon *Robin Hoode*, than upon *Apollo* or the *Muſes*. Tox. Over earneſt ſhootinge ſurelye I will not over earneſtlye defende, for I ever thought ſhootinge ſhoulde be a wayter upon learnynge, not a miſtreſs over learnynge. Yet this I marveile not a little at, that ye thincke a man with a bowe on his backe is more like *Robin Hoodes* ſervaunte, than *Apollos*, ſeinge that *Apollo* himſelfe, in [8] *Alceſtis* of *Euripides*, which tragedye you redde openlye not longe ago, in a manner glorifyeth, ſayinge this verſe.

It is my wont alwayes my bowe with me to beare.

Therefore a learned man ought not to much to be aſhamed to beare that ſometime which *Apollo* God

[8] *Eurip. in Alceſt.*

of

of learninge himfelfe was not afhamed always to
bear. And becaufe ye woulde have a man wayte
upon the *Mufes*, and not at all meddle with fhootinge ; I marveile that you do not remember how
that the nine *Mufes* their felfe as foone as they were
borne, were put to norfe to a lady called *Euphemis*,
which had a fonne named *Erotus*, with whom the
nine *Mufes*, for his excellent fhootinge, kepte
evermore companye withall, and ufed dailye to
fhoote together in the mounte *Parnaffus :* and at
laft it chaunced this *Erotus* to dye, whofe death the
Mufes lamented greatlye, and fell all upon theyr
knees fore *Jupiter* theyr father, and, at theyr requeft, *Erotus*, for fhootinge with the *Mufes* on
earth, was made a figne, and called *Sagittarius* in
heaven. Therefore you fee that if *Apollo* and the
Mufes eyther were examples indeede, or onlye
fayned of wyfe men to be examples of learninge,
honeft fhootinge may well enoughe be companion
with honeft ftudye. PHI. Well, *Toxophile*, if
you have no ftronger defence of fhootinge than
poetes, I feare if your companions which love
fhootinge heard you, they would thincke you made
it but a triflinge and fablinge matter, rather than
any other man that loveth not fhootinge coulde
be perfwaded by this reafon to love it. Tox.

F   Even

Even as I am not ſo fonde but I knowe that theſe
be fables, ſo I am ſure you be not ſo ignorante,
but you know what ſuch noble wittes as the poetes
had ment by ſuch matters, which oftentimes, under
the covering of a fable, do hyde and wrappe in
goodlye preceptes of philoſophie, with the true
judgement of thinges. Whiche to be true ſpecially
in *Homer* and *Euripides*, *Plato*, *Ariſtotle*, and *Ga-*
lene, plainlye do ſhewe : when throughe all theyr
workes (in a manner) they determine all controver-
ſies by theſe two poetes, and ſuch like authorityes.
Therefore if in this matter I ſeeme to fable, and
nothing prove, I am content you judge ſo on me,
ſeinge the ſame judgement ſhall condemne with me
Plato, *Ariſtotle*, and *Galene*, whom in that errour
I am well content to followe. If theſe old examples prove nothinge for ſhootinge, what ſaye you
to theſe ? that the beſt learned and ſageſt men in
this realme which be now alive, both love ſhootinge, and uſe ſhootinge, as the beſt learned biſhops
that be : amonges whom, *Philologe*, yourſelfe knowe
four or five, which as in all good learninge, vertue
and ſageneſſe, they geve other men example what
thinge they ſhould do, even ſo by their ſhootinge
they plainlye ſhewe what honeſt paſtime other men
geven to learninge may honeſtlye uſe. That earneſt
ſtudye

studye muſt be recreated with ſome paſtime, ſuf-
ficientlye I have proved afore, both by reaſon and
authoritye of the beſt learned men that ever wrote.
Then ſeinge paſtimes be lawfull, the moſt fitteſt
for learninge is to be ſought for. A paſtime, ſayth
Ariſtotle, muſt be like a medicine. Medicines
ſtande by contraryes; therefore, the nature of ſtudy-
inge conſidered, the fitteſt paſtime ſhall ſoon appeare. In ſtudye every part of the bodye is idle,
which thinge cauſeth groſſe and cold humours to
gather together and vexe ſcholers very much, the
minde is altogether bent and ſette on work: a paſtime then muſt be had where everye part of the
bodye muſt be laboured to ſeparate and leſſen ſuch
humours withall, the minde muſt be unbent, to gather and fetch againe his quickneſs withall. Thus
paſtimes for the minde onelye, be nothinge fitte
for ſtudentes, becauſe the bodye, which is moſt
hurt by ſtudye, ſhoulde take no profite at all thereat.
This knewe *Eraſmus* very well, when he was here in
Cambrige: which when he had been ſore at his booke
(as *Garret* our booke-bynder has verye oft told me)
for lacke of better exerciſe, would take his horſe,
and ryde about the market hill, and come againe.
If a ſcholer ſhould uſe bowles or tennyes, the labour is ſo vehement and unequal, which is con-

demned

demned of *Galene*; the example very ill for other men, when by fo manye actes they be made unlawfull. Runninge, leapinge, and coytinge be to vile for fcholers, and not fitte by *Ariftotles* judgement: walkinge alone in the field hath no token of courage in it, a paftime like a fingle man that is neither flefhe nor fifhe. Therefore if a man would have a paftime holfome and equall for every part of his bodye, pleafant and full of courage for the minde, not vile and unhoneft to geve ill example to laye men, not kept in gardines and corners, not lurkinge on the night and in holes, but evermore in the face of men, eyther to rebuke it when it doth ill, or els to teftifye on it when it doth well; let him feeke chieflye of all other for fhootinge. PHI. Such common paftimes as men commonly do ufe, I will not greatlye allowe to be fitte for fcholers, feinge they may ufe fuch exercifes very well (I fuppofe) as [9] *Galen* himfelfe doth allow. TOX. Thefe exercifes, I remember very well, for I redde them within thefe two dayes, of of the which fome be thefe: to runne up and downe an hill, to clyme up a longe powle, or a rope, and there hange a while, to holde a man by his armes and wave with his heeles, muche like the

[9] Gal. de Santuend. 2.

paftime

paftime that boyes ufe in the churche, when theyr
mafter is awaye, to fwinge and totter in a belrope :
to make a fifte, and ftretche out both his armes,
and fo ftand like a roode. To go on a mans tip-
toes, ftretchinge out the one of his armes forward,
the other backeward, whiche, if he blered out his
tongue alfo, might be thoughte to dance anticke
verye properlye. To tumble over and over, to
toppe over tayle : to fet backe to backe, and fee
who can heave an others heeles higheft, wyth other
much like : which exercifes furely mufte needes be
naturall, becaufe they be fo childifhe, and they maye
be alfo holfome for the bodye, but furelye as for
pleafure to the minde, or honeftye in the doinge of
them, they be as like fhootinge as *Yorke* is foule
Sutton. Therefore to loke on all paftimes and exercifes holefome for the bodye, pleafaunt for the
minde, comlye for every man to do, honeft for all
other to loke on, profitable to be fet by of every
man, worthy to be rebuked of no man, fitte for
all ages, perfons and places, onlye fhootinge fhall
appeare, wherein all thefe commodities may be
founde. PHI. To graunt, *Toxophile*, that ftu-
dentes may at times convenient ufe fhootinge as
moft holefome and honeft paftime : yet to do as
fome do, to fhoote hourelye, dailye, weekely, and

in

in a manner the whole yeare, neyther I can prayſe, nor any wyſe man will allowe, nor you yourſelfe can honeſtly defend.   Tox. Surelye, *Philologe*, I am very glad to ſee you come to that point that moſt lyeth in your ſtomache, and greveth you and others ſo muche. But I truſt, after I have ſayde my minde in this matter, you ſhall confeſſe your ſelfe, that you do rebuke this thinge more than ye neede, rather than you ſhall finde that any man maye ſpende by anye poſſibilitye, more time in ſhootinge then he oughte. For firſt and formoſt, the hole time is divided into two partes, the daye and the nighte: whereof the nighte maye be bothe occupyed in manye honeſt buſineſſes, and alſo ſpente in much unthriftineſſe, but in no wyſe it can be applyed to ſhootinge. And here you ſee that halfe our time, graunted to all other thinges in a manner both good and ill, is at one ſwappe quite taken awaye from ſhootinge. Now let us go forwarde, and ſee howe much of halfe this time of ours is ſpent in ſhootinge. The whole yeare is divided into four partes, ſpringe-time, ſommer, faule of the leafe, and winter. Whereof the winter, for the roughneſſe of it, is cleane taken away from ſhootinge: except it be one daye amonges twenty, or one yeare amonges forty. In ſommer,

for

for the fervent heate, a man may faye likewife;
excepte it be fome time againft night. Nowe then
fpringe time and faule of the leafe, be thofe which
we abufe in fhootinge.

But if we confider howe mutable and change-
able the weather is in thofe feafons, and howe that
Ariftotle himfelfe fayth, that moft part of rayne
fauleth in thefe two times; we fhall well perceive,
that where a man would fhoote one daye, he fhall
be fayne to leave of four. Nowe when time itfelfe
graunteth us but a little fpace to fhoote in, let us
fee if fhootinge be not hindered amonges all kindes
of men as muche other wayes.

Firft, younge children ufe not; younge men,
for fear of them whom they be under, too muche
dare not; fage men, for other greater bufines, will
not; aged men, for lacke of ftrengthe, cannot;
riche men, for covetoufneffe fake, care not; poore
men, for coft and charge, may not; maifters, for
theyr houfhold kepinge, heede not; fervauntes,
kept in by theyr maifters, verye oft fhall not;
craftefmen, for gettinge of their lyvinge, very muche
leyfure have not; and many there be that oft be-
ginnes, but, for inaptneffe, proves not; and moft
of

of all, which when they be ſhooters geve it over and liſt not: So that generallye men everye where, for one or other conſideration, much ſhootinge uſe not. Therefore theſe two thinges, ſtraytneſſe of time, and everye mans trade of lyvinge, are the cauſes that ſo fewe men ſhotes, as you may ſee in this greate towne, where as there be a thouſand good mennes bodyes, yet ſcarce ten that uſeth anye greate ſhootinge. And thoſe whom you ſee ſhoote the moſt, with how manye thinges are they drawen, or rather driven, from ſhootinge. For firſt, as it is manye a yeare or they begin to be great ſhooters, even ſo the great heate of ſhootinge is gone within a yeare or two: as you knowe diverſe, *Philologe*, yourſelfe, which were ſome time the beſt ſhooters, and now they be the beſt ſtudentes.

If a man faule ſicke, farewell ſhootinge, maye fortune as longe as he lyveth. If he have a wrentche, or have taken colde in his arme, he maye hange uppe his bowe (I warrant you) for a ſeaſon. A litle blayne, a ſmall cutte, yea a ſilye poore worme in his finger, maye keepe him from ſhootinge well enoughe. Breakinge and ill lucke in bowes I will paſſe over, with an hundred mo ſere thinges, which chaunceth every day to them that

ſhoote

fhoote moft, whereof the leaft of them maye compell a man to leave fhootinge. And thefe thinges
be fo true and evident, that it is impoffible eyther
for me craftilye to fayne them, or els for you juft-
lye to denye them. Then feinge how manye hundred thinges are required altogether to geve a man
leave to fhoote, and any one of them denyed, a
man cannot fhoote ; and feeinge every one of them
may chaunce, and doth chaunce every daye, I
marveile any wyfe man will thincke it poffible, that
any great time can be fpent in fhootinge at all.

PHI. If this be true that you faye, *Toxophile*,
and in very dede, I can denye nothinge of it, I
merveile greatly how it chaunceth, that thofe which
ufe fhootinge be fo much marked of men, and oft
times blamed for it, and that in a manner as much
as thofe which playe at [10] cardes and dyfe. And
I fhall tell you what I hearde fpoken of the fame
matter. A man, no fhooter, (not longe ago)
would defend playing at cardes and dyfe, if it were
honeftlye ufed, to be as honeft paftime as your
fhootinge : for he layed for him, that a man might
playe for a litle at cardes and dyfe, and alfo a man
might fhoote away all that ever he had. He fayde

[10] Cardes and Dyfe.

G

a payre

a payre of cardes coſt not paſt two pence, and that
they neded not ſo much reparation as bowe and
ſhaftes, they would never hurte a mans hande, nor
never weare his gere. A man ſhould never ſlea a
man with ſhootinge wyde at the cardes. In wete
and drye, hote and colde, they woulde never forſake a man, he ſhewed what great varietye there is
in them for every mans capacity : if one game were
hard, he might eaſily learne an other : if a man
have a good game, there is great pleaſure in it : if
he have an ill game, the payne is ſhort, for he may
ſone geve it over, and hope for a better : with
many other mo reaſons. But at the laſt he con-
cluded, that betwixte playinge and ſhootinge, well
uſed or ill uſed, there was no difference : but that
there was leſſe coſte and trouble, and a great deale
more pleaſure in playinge, than in ſhootinge.

Tox. I cannot denye, but ſhootinge (as all
other good thinges) may be abuſed. And good
thinges ungodly uſed, are not good, ſayth an honourable biſhoppe in an earneſter matter than this
is : yet we muſt be ware that we laye not mennes
faultes upon the thinge which is not worthy, for
ſo nothinge ſhould be good. And as for ſhootinge, it is blamed and marked of men for that
                                                          thing

thing (as I have fayd before) which fhould be rather a token of honeftye to prayfe it, then anye
figne of noughtineffe to difalowe it, and that is becaufe it is in everye mans fight; it feeketh no corners,
it hydeth it not : if there be never fo litle faulte in
it, every man feeth it, it accufeth itfelfe.   For one
houre fpente in fhootinge is more feene, and further talked of, than twenty nights fpent in dyfinge,
even as a little white ftone is feene amonges three
hundred blacke.   Of thefe that blame fhootinge
and fhooters, I will faye no more at this time but
this, that befide that they ftoppe and hinder fhootinge, which the ftatutes would have forwarde, they
be not much unlike in this pointe to *Wyll Sommer*
the Kinges foole, which fmiteth him that ftandeth
always before his face, be he never fo worfhipfull
a man, and never greatlye lokes for him which
lurkes behinde an other mans backe, that hurte
him in deede.

But to him that compared gaminge with fhootinge fomewhat will I aunfwere, and becaufe he
wente afore me in a comparifon : and comparifons,
fayth learned men, make plaine matters : I will
furelye followe him in the fame.   Honefte thinges
(fayth

(fayth [1] *Plato*) be known from unhoneft thinges
by this difference, unhoneftye hath ever prefent
pleafure in it, havinge neyther good pretence goinge
before, nor yet anye profite followinge after : which
fayinge defcryeth generallye, both the nature of
fhootinge and gaminge, which is good, and which
is evill, verye well.

Gaminge hath joined with it a vaine prefente
pleafure, but there followeth loffe of name, loffe
of goods, and winninge of an hundred gowtye,
dropfye, difeafes, as everye man can tell.   Shootinge
is a paynfull paftime, whereof followeth health of
bodye, quickneffe of witte, habilitye to defende our
country, as our ennemyes can bear recorde.

Loth I am to compare thefe thinges together,
and yet I do it not becaufe there is anye comparifon at all betwixte them, but thereby a man fhall
fee how good the one is, how evill the other.   For
I thincke there is fcarce fo much contrarioufnefs
betwixt hotte and cold, vertue and vice, as is betwixte thefe two thinges : For whatfoever is in the
one, the cleane contrarye is in the other, as fhall
plainlye appere, if we confider both theyr begin-

[1] In Phedro.

ninges,

ninges, theyr encreasinges, theyr fruites, and theyr
endes, which I will soone ridde over.

The first bringer into the worlde of shootinge, was
[2] *Apollo*, which for his wysedome, and greate commodityes, broughte amonges men by him, was
esteemed worthye to be counted as a God in heaven.

Dysinge surelye is a bastard borne, because it is
sayde to have two fathers, and yet both nought:
the one was an ungratious God, called [3] *Theuth*,
which, for his noughtinesse, came never in other
Goddes companyes, and therefore *Homer* doth de-
spise once to name him in all his workes. The
other was a [4] *Lydian* borne, which people for such
games, and other unthriftinesse, as bowlinge and
hauntinge of tavernes, have bene ever had in most
vile reputation in all storyes and writers.

The fosterer of shootinge is Labour, that companion of vertue, the mainteyner of honestye, the
encrease of healthe and wealthinesse, which admit-
teth nothinge, in a manner, into his companye
that standeth not with vertue and honestye; and
therefore sayth the olde Poete *Epichermus* verye

[2] Pla. in Tim. [3] Plato in Phedro. [4] Herod. in Clio.
pretelye

pretelye in ⁵ *Zenophon*, that God felleth vertue, and all other good thinges to men for labour. The nource of dyse and cardes, is werisome idlenesse, enemye of vertue, the drowner of youthe, that taryeth in it, and, as *Chaucer* doth say verye well in the Parsons Tale, the grene path waye to hell, havinge this thinge appropriate unto it, that whereas other vices have some cloke of honestye, onlye idlenesʃ can neyther do well, nor yet thincke well. Againe; ʃhootinge hath two tutours to loke upon it, out of whose companye ʃhootinge never ʃtirreth, the one called day-light, the other open place, which two kepe ʃhootinge from evill companye, and ʃuffer it not to have to much ʃwinge, but ever more kepeth it under awe, that it dare do nothinge in the open face of the world, but that which is good and honeʃt. Lykewiʃe, dyʃinge and cardinge have two tutours, the one named Solitariouʃneʃʃe, which lurketh in holes and corners, the other called Night, an ungratious cover of noughtineʃʃe, which two thinges be very inkepers and receyvers of all noughtineʃʃe and noughtye thinges, and thereto they be in a manner ordayned by nature. For, in the night time and in corners, ʃpirites and theeves, rattes and miʃe, toodes and oules, night crowes

⁵ Xen de dict. & fact. Soc.

and poulcattes, foxes and * foumardes, with all
other vermine, and noyſome beaſtes, uſe moſt ſtyr-
ringe; when in the day-light, and in open places,
which be ordayned of God for honeſt thinges, they
dare not ones come, which thinge *Euripides* noteth
very well, ſayinge,

Ill thinges the night, good thinges the daye doth haunt and uſe.   Iph. in Tau.

Companions of ſhootinge, by providentneſs,
good heede geving, true meetinge, honeſt compa-
riſon, which thinges agree with vertue verye well.
Cardinge and dyſinge have a ſort of good felowes
alſo, goinge commonlye in theyr companye, as
blinde fortune, ſtumblinge chaunce, ſpittle lucke,
falſe dealinge, craftye conveyaunce, brainleſſe brawl-
inge, falſe forſwearinge, which good fellowes will
ſone take a man by the ſleve, and cauſe him take
his inne, ſome with beggary, ſome with goute and
dropſye, ſome with thefte and robbery, and ſeldome they will leave a man before he come eyther
to hanginge, or els ſome other extreme myſerye.
To make an ende, how ſhootinge by all mennes
lawes hath bene alowed, cardinge and dyſinge by
all mennes judgementes condempned, I neede not
ſhewe, the matter is ſo plaine .

* Foumards, by others called Fumarts, are, we believe, what are now called
more commonly Stoats.

Therefore

Therefore, when the *Lydians* shall invente better thinges than *Apollo*, when slouthe and ydlenefs
shall encreafe vertue more than laboure, when the
night and lurkinge corners geveth leffe occafion to
unthriftineffe, than light day and openneſs, then
shall shootinge, and fuch gaminge, be in some comparifon like. Yet even, as I do not shewe all the
goodneſs which is in shootinge, when I prove it
standeth by the fame thinges that vertue itfelfe
standeth by, as brought in by gods, or god-like
men, foftered by labour, committed to the fave-
garde of light and openneffe, accompanyed with
provifion and diligence, loved and allowed by everye
good mans fentence: even likewife do I not open
halfe the naughtineffe which is in cardinge and dyfinge, when I shewe how they are borne of a de-
fperate mother, nourished in idleneffe, encreafed
by lycence of nighte and corners, accompanyed
with fortune, chaunce, deceyte, and craftineffe:
condemned and banished by all lawes and judgementes.

For if I woulde enter to defcribe the monftruouf-
neffe of it, I should rather wander in it, it is fo
brode, than have anye readye paffage to the ende
of the matter: whofe horribleneffe is fo large, that
it

it paſſed the eloquence of our [6] *Engliſhe Homer* to compaſſe it : yet becauſe I ever thoughte his ſayinges to have as much authoritye as eyther *Sophocles* or *Euripides* in *Greeke*, therefore gladlye do I remember theſe verſes of his.

> Haſardry is verye mother of leſinges,
> And of deceyte, and curſed ſweringes.
> Blaſphemye of Chriſt, mans ſlaughter, and waſte alſo!
> Of catel, of tyme, of other thinges mo.

Mother of * leſinges.] True it maye be called ſo, if a man conſider how many wayes and how many thinges he loſeth thereby; for firſt, he loſeth his goodes, he loſeth his time, he loſeth quickneſſe of witte, and all good luſte to other thinges; he loſeth honeſt companye, he loſeth his good name and eſtimation, and at laſt, if he leave it not, loſeth God, and heaven and all : and, inſteede of theſe thinges, winneth at length eyther hanginge or hell.

And of deceyte.] I trowe, if I ſhould not lye, there is not halfe ſo much crafte uſed in no one thinge in the world, as in this curſed thinge. What falſe dyſe uſe they? As dyſe ſtopped with quick ſilver and heares, dyſe of vauntage, flattes, gourdes

[6] Chaucer.

* We doubt whether our authour has not miſtaken the ſenſe of Chaucer, we rather take leſinges to be lies than loſſes.

H   to

to chop and chaunge when they lifte, to let the true dyfe fall under the table, and fo take up the falfe, and if they be true dyfe, what fhift will they make to fet the one of them with flydinge, with cogginge, with foyftinge, with coytinge as they call it. How will they ufe thefe fhiftes, when they get a plaine man that cannot fkill of them? how will they go about, if they perceive an honeft man have moneye, which lift not playe, to provoke him to playe? They will feeke his companye, they will let him pay noughte, yea, and as I hearde a man ones faye that he did, they will fende for him to fome houfe, and fpende perchaunce a crowne on him, and, at laft, will one begin to faye: What my mafters, what fhall we do? fhall every man playe his twelve-pence whiles an apple rofte in the fyre, and then we will drincke and departe: Naye, will an other faye, (as falfe as he) you cannot leave when you begin, and therefore I will not playe: but if you will gage, that every man, as he hath loft his twelve-pence, fhall fit downe, I am con-tente, for furelye I would winne no mannes mo-neye here, but even as much as woulde paye for my fupper. Then fpeaketh the thirde, to the ho-nefte man that thoughte not to playe, What? will you playe your twelve-pence? If he excufe him;

Tufh

Tuſh man, will the other ſaye, ſticke not in honeſte companye for twelve-pence; I will beare your
halfe, and here is my moneye.

Nowe all this is to make him to beginne, for
they knowe if he be ones in, and be a loſer, that
he will not ſtick at his twelve-pence, but hopeth
ever to get it againe, while perhappes he loſe all.
Than everye one of them ſetteth his ſhiftes abroache,
ſome with falſe dyſe, ſome with ſettling of dyſe,
ſome with having outelandiſhe ſilver coynes guilded,
to put awaye at a time for good golde. Than if
there come a thinge in controverſye, muſt you be
judged by the table, and than farewell the honeſt
mans parte, for he is borne downe on every ſyde.

Nowe, Sir, beſyde all theſe thinges, they have
certaine termes (as a man woulde ſaye) appropriate
to theyr playinge: whereby they will drawe a mannes
moneye, but paye none, which they call barres, that
ſurelye he that knoweth them not maye ſoone be debarred of all that ever he hath, before he learne them.
If a plaine man loſe, as he ſhall do ever, or els it is
a wonder, then the game is ſo deviliſh, that he can
never leave: for vaine hope, (which hope, ſayth
Euripides,

[7] *Euripides,* deſtroyeth manye a man, and cittye)
driveth him on ſo farre, that he can never return
backe, until he be ſo light that he neede feare no
theeves by the waye. Nowe if a ſimple man happen once in his life to winne of ſuch players, than
will they eyther entreate him to keepe them companye whiles he hath loſt all againe, or els they
will uſe the moſt devilyſhe faſhion of all, for one
of the players that ſtandeth next him ſhall have a
payre of falſe dyſe, and caſt them out upon the
bourde, the honeſt man ſhall take them and caſt
them as he did the other, the thirde ſhall eſpye
them to be falſe dyſe, and ſhall crye oute harde,
with all the othes under God, that he has falſelye
wonne theyr moneye, and than there is nothinge
but houlde thy throte from my dagger; everye man
layeth hande on the ſimple man, and taketh all
theyr money from him, and his owne alſo, thinking himſelfe well, that he eſcapeth with his life.

Curſed ſwerynge blaſphemye of Chriſte.] Theſe
halfe verſes *Chaucer,* in another place, more at
large doth well ſet out, and very livelye expreſſe,
ſayinge.

> Fy by Goddes precious hart and his nayles,
> And by the bloud of Chriſte, that is in Hales,

[7] In Suppli.

Seven

Seven is my chaunce. and thine is cinke and treye,
Ey Goddes armes, if thou falfelye playe,
This dagger fhall thoroughe thine harte go,
This fruite commeth of the beched boones two,
Forfweringe, ire, falfeneffe, and homicide, &c.

Thoughe thefe verfes be verye earneftlye written, yet they do not halfe fo grifelye fet out the
horiblenesse of blafphemye, which fuch gammers
ufe, as it is indeede, and as I have heard myfelfe.
For no man can write a thinge fo earneftlye, as
whan it is fpoken with gefture, as learned men,
you knowe, do faye. Howe will you thincke that
fuche furioufneffe, with woode countenaunce, and
brenninge eyes, with ftaringe and bragginge, with
hart redye to leape out of the bellye for fwellinge,
can be expreffed the tenthe part, to the uttermoft.
Two men I heard myfelfe, whofe fayinges be farre
more grifelye, than *Chaucers* verfes. One, when
he had lofte his moneye, fware me God from top
to the toe with one breathe, that he had loft all
his moneye for lacke of fweringe: the other lofinge
his moneye, and heapinge othes upon othes one
in anothers necke, moft horrible, and not fpeakable, was rebuked of an honeft man which ftoode
by for fo doinge, he by and by, ftaringe him in
the face, and clappinge his fifte, with all his moneye he had, upon the boarde, fware me by the
                                                    flefhe

fleſhe of God, that, if ſweringe would helpe him
but one ace, he would not leave one pece of God
unſworne, neyther within nor without. The remembraunce of this blaſphemye, *Philologe*, doth
make me quake at the hart, and therefore I will
ſpeake no more of it.

And ſo to conclude with ſuch gaminge, I thincke
there no ungratiouſneſſe in all this world, that
carieth a man ſo farre from God, as this fault doth.
And if there were anye ſo deſperate a perſon, that
would begin his hell in earth, I trowe he ſhould
not finde hell more like hell itſelfe, than the life of
of thoſe men is, which daily haunt and uſe ſuch
ungratious games.   PHI. You handle this gere
indeede; and I ſuppoſe, if you had bene a prentice
at ſuch games, you could not have ſayd more of
them than you have done, and by like you have
had ſomewhat to do with them.   TOX. Indede,
you may honeſtlye gather that I hate them greatly, in
that I ſpeak againſt them : not that I have uſed them
greatly in that I ſpeake of them. For things
be knowen divers wayes, as *Socrates* (you know)
doth prove in *Alcibiades*. And if every man ſhould
be that, that he ſpeaketh or wryteth upon, then
ſhould *Homer* have bene the beſt captaine, moſt
cowarde,

còwarde, hardye, haftye, wyfe and woode, fage
and fimple: and *Terence* an oulde man and a younge,
an honeft man and a bawde: with fuch like.
Surelye every man ought to praye to God dailye,
to kepe them from fuch unthriftineffe, and fpeciallye all the youth of *Englande*: for what youth
doth begin, a man will folowe commonlye, even
to his dying day: which thinge *Adraſtus*, in *Euripides*, pretelye doth expreſſe, fayinge:

> What thing a man in tender age hath moſt in ure,
> That fame to death alwayes to kepe he fhall be fure.
> Therefore in age who greatly longes good fruite to mowe,
> In youth he muſt himfelfe applye good feede to fowe.   Euripides in Suppli.

For the foundation of youthe well fet (as *Plato*
doth faye) the whole bodye of the common wealthe
fhall flourifhe thereafter. If the younge tree growe
croked, when it is oulde a man fhall rather breake
it than ftreight it. And I thincke there is no one
thing that crokes youthe more then fuch unlawful
games. Nor let no man faye, if they be honeftly
ufed they do no harme. For how can that paftime which neyther exercifeth the bodye with any
honeft labour, nor yet the minde with any honeft
thinckinge, have any honeftye joined with it? Nor
let no man affure himfelfe that he can ufe it honeftlye: for if he ftand therein, he may fortune
have

have a faule, the thinge is more flipperye than he knoweth of. A man maye (I graunt) fit on a brante hill fide, but if geve never fo little forward, he cannot ftoppe, though he would never fo fayne, but he muft needes runne head-long, he knoweth not how farre. What honeft pretences vayne pleafure layeth daily (as it were entifementes or baytes, to pull men forwarde withall) *Homer* doth well fhewe, by the *Sirenes* and *Circe*. And amonges all in that fhippe, there was but one *Ulyffes*, and yet he had done to as the other did, if a goddeffe had not taughte him ; and fo likewife, I thincke, they be eafye to nomber, which paffe by playinge honeftly, except the grace of God fave and keep them. Therefore they that will not go to farre in playinge, let them folowe this counfell of the Poet :

Stoppe the beginninges.

Phi. Well, or you go any further, I praye you tell me this one thinge : Doo you fpeake againft meane mennes playinge onlye, or againft greate mennes playinge to, or put you any difference betwixte them ? Tox. If I fhould excufe myfelfe herein, and fay that I fpake of the one and not of the other, I fear leafte I fhoulde as fondlye excufe myfelfe, as a certaine preacher did, whom I heard
upon

upon a time speake against many abuses, (as he sayde) and, at last, he spake against candelles, and then, he fearinge, least some men would have bene angrye and offended with him, Naye, sayth he, you must take me as I meane : I speake not against greate candelles, but against litle candelles, for they be not all one (quoth he) I promise you ; and so everye man laughed him to scorne.

Indeede, as for great men, and great mennes matters, I list not greatlye to meddle. Yet this I would wishe, that all great men in *Englande* had redde over diligently the Pardoners Tale in *Chaucer,* and there they shoulde perceive and see, how muche such games stande with their worshippe, how great soever they be. What great men do, be it good or ill, meane men commonlye love to followe, as many learned men in many places do saye, and dailye experience doth plainlye shewe, in costlye apparell and other like matters.

Therefore, seinge that lordes be lanternes to lead the life of meane men, by their example, either to goodnesse or badnesse, to whether soever they liste : and seinge also they have libertye to list what they will, I praye God they have will to list

I   that

that which is good; and as for their playing, I will
make an ende with this sayinge of *Chaucer*.

> Lordes might finde them other maner of playe,
> Honest ynough to dreve the daye awaye.

But to be short, the best medicine for all sortes
of men, both highe and lowe, younge and oulde,
to put away such unlawful games is by the contrarye, likewise as all *Phisitions* do allowe in *Phi-
sicke*. So let youthe, instede of such unlawful
games, which stande by ydlenesse, by solitarinesse,
and corners, by night and darknesse, by fortune
and chaunce, by craft and subtiltye, use such pastimes as stand by labour: upon the day light, in
open sighte of men, havinge such an ende as is
come to by cunninge, rather than by craft: and
so should virtue encrease, and vice decaye. For
contrarye pastimes, must nedes worke contrarye
mindes in men, as all other contrarye thinges do.

And thus we see, *Philologe*, that shootinge is not
onlye the most holesome exercise for the bodye, the
most honest pastime for the minde, and that for all
sortes of men: but also it is a most redye medycine, to purge the whole realme of such pestilent
gaminge, wherewith manye times it is sore troubled,
and ill at ease.

PHI.

PHI. The more honeſtye you have proved by ſhootinge, *Toxophile,* and the more you have per-ſuaded me to love it, ſo much· trulye the ſoryer have you made me with this laſte ſentence of yours, whereby you plainly prove that a man may not greatly uſe it. For if ſhootinge be a medycine (as you ſaye that it is) it may not be uſed very oft, leſt a man ſhould hurte himſelfe withall, as medycines much occupyed doo. For *Ariſtotle* himſelfe ſayth, that medycines be not meate to live withall : and thus ſhootinge, by the ſame reaſon, maye not be much occupyed.   Tox. You playe your olde wontes, *Philologe,* in dalyinge with other mennes wittes, not ſo much to prove your owne matter, as to prove what other men can ſaye.   But where you thincke that I take away much uſe of ſhootinge, in lykening it to a medycine : becauſe men uſe not medycines everye daye, for ſo ſhould theyr bodyes be hurte : I rather prove daily uſe of ſhootinge thereby. For although *Ariſtotle* ſayth that ſome medycines be no meate to live withal, which is true : yet [8] *Hippocrates* ſayth our dailye meates be medycines, to withſtand evill withal, which is as true, for he maketh two kindes of medycines, one our meate that we uſe dailye, which purgeth ſoft-

[8] Hippoc. de med. purg.

lye

lye and flowlye, and in this fimilitude maye fhootinge be called a medycine, wherewith dailye a man
maye purge and take away all unlawful defires to
other unlawful paftimes, as I proved before. The
other is a quicke purginge medycine, and feldomer
to be occupyed, except the matter be greater, and
I could defcribe the nature of a quicke medycine,
which fhould within a while purge and plucke out
all the unthriftye games in the realme, through
which the common wealthe oftentimes is ficke.
For not onlye good quicke wittes to learninge be
thereby broughte oute of frame, and quite marred,
but alfo manly wittes, eyther to attempt matters
of high courage in warre time, or elfe to atchieve
matters of weight and wyfdome in peace time, be
made thereby very quafye and faynte. For loke
through all hiftories written in *Greeke*, *Latine*, or
other language, and you fhall never finde that
realme profper in the whiche fuch ydle paftimes are
ufed. As concerninge the medycine, althoughe
fome would be mifcontent, if they heard me meddle anye thinge with it : yet, betwixt you and me
here alone, I maye the boldlyer faye my fantafye,
and the rather becaufe I will onlye wifh for it,
which ftandeth with honefty, not determine of it,
which belongeth to authoritye. The medycine is
this,

this, that would to God and the Prince, all thefe
unthriftye ydle paftimes, which be very bugges that
the 9 *Pfalme* meaneth on, walking on the night
and in corners, were made felonye, and fome of
that punifhment ordayned for them, which is appointed for the forgers and falfifyers of the King's
coyne. Which punifhment is not by me now invented, but long ago, by the mofte noble oratour
10 *Demofthenes*, which marveileth greatlye that
death is appoinsed for falfifyers and forgers of the
coyne, and not as greate punifhmente ordayned
for them, which by their meanes forges and falfi-
fyes the common wealth. And I fuppofe that there
is no one thinge that changeth foner the golden
filver wittes of men into copperye and braffye wayes,
then dyfinge and fuch unlawfull paftimes.

And this quicke medycine, I believe, woulde fo
throwlye purge them, that the daily medycines, as
fhootinge and other paftimes joyned with honeft
labour, fhoulde eafelyer withftand them. PHI.
The excellent commodities of fhootinge in peace
time, *Toxophile*, you have verye well and fuffici-
ently declared. Whereby you have fo perfuaded
me, that God willinge, hereafter I will both love it

9 Pfalme 90.   10 Demoft. contra Leptinem.
                                          the

the better, and alfo ufe it the ofter. For as much
as I can gather of all this communication of ours,
the tongue, the nofe, the handes, and the feete,
be no fitter members, or inftrumentes for the bodye
of a man, than is fhootinge for the hole body of
the realme. God hath made the partes of men
which be beft and moft neceffarye, to ferve, not
for one purpofe onlye, but for manye: as the tongue
for fpeakinge and taftinge, the nofe for fmellinge,
and alfo for avoydinge all excrementes, which faule
out of the head, the handes for receiving of good
thinges, and for puttinge of all harmfull thinges
from the bodye. So fhootinge is an exercife of
healthe, a paftime of honefte pleafure, and fuch one
alfo that ftoppeth and avoydeth all noyfome games,
gathered and encreafed by ill rule, as noughtye humours be, which hurt and corrupte fore that parte
of the realme, wherein they do remayne. But
nowe if you can fhewe but halfe fo muche profite
in warre of fhootinge, as you have proved pleafure in peace, then will I furelye judge that there
be fewe thinges that have fo manifolde commodities and ufes joyned unto them as it hath.

Tox. The upper hand in warre, next the goodneffe of God, (of whom all victory commeth, as
Scripture

Scripture fayth) [1] ftandeth chieflye in three thinges:
in the wifedome of the Prince, in the fleightes and
pollicies of the captaynes, and in the ftrengthe and
cherefull forwardneffe of the fouldiours. A Prince
in his harte mufte be full of mercye and peace, a
vertue moft pleafaunt to Chrift, moft agreeable to
mans nature, moft profitable for riche and poore;
for then the riche man enjoyeth with great pleafure
the which he hath: the poore may obtaine with
his labour, that which he lacketh. And althoughe
there is nothinge worfe then * warre, whereof it
taketh his name, throughe the which great men be
in daunger, meane men without fuccour; riche
men in feare, becaufe they have fomewhat; poore
men in care, becaufe they have nothinge; and
every man in doubt and miferye: yet it is a civill
medycine, wherewith a Prince may, from the bodye
of his common wealthe, put off that danger which
may faule: or els recover againe, whatfoever it hath
lofte. And therefore, as *Ifocrates* doth faye, a
Prince muft be a warriour in two thinges, in cunninge and knowledge of all fleightes and feates of
warre, and in havinge all neceffary habilimentes be-

[1] Mach. 5. 3.

* War is an old word, ftill ufed in fome counties for worfe, and ASCHAM
fuppofes that war or hoftility is fo named, becaufe it is war or worfe than
peace.

longinge

longinge to the fame. Which matter to entreate at large, were over longe at this time to declare, and over much for my learninge to perfourme.

After the wifedome of the Prince, are valiant captaines moft neceffarye in warre, whofe office and dutye is to knowe all fleightes and pollicies for all kindes of warre, which they may learne two wayes, eyther in dailye folowinge and haunttinge the warres, or els, becaufe wyfedome boughte with ftripes is manye times over coftlye, they may beftow fome time in *Vegetius*, which entreateth fuch matters in *Latine* metelye well, or rather in *Polyenus*, and *Leo* the Emperour, which fetteth oute all pollicies and duties of captaines in the *Greeke* tongue verye excellentlye. But chieflye I would wifhe, and (if I were of authoritye) I woulde counfell all the younge gentlemen of this realme, never to laye out of their hands two authors, *Zenophon* in *Greeke*, and *Cæfar* in *Latine*, wherein they fhould folow noble *Scipio Africanus*, as [2] *Tullie* doth fay: in which two authors, befydes eloquence, a thinge moft neceffarye of all other for a captaine, they fhould learne the hole courfe of warre, which thofe two noble men did not more wifelye write for other

[2] De Sen.

men

men to learne, than they did manfully exercife in
the field, for other men to folowe.

The ftrengthe of warre lyeth in the fouldiour,
whofe chiefe prayfe and vertue is [3] obedience towarde his captaine, fayth [4] *Plato*. And [5] *Zenophon*, being a gentyle author, moft chriftianlye doth
faye, even by thefe wordes, that that fouldiour
which firft ferveth God, and then obeyeth his captaine, maye boldlye, with all courage, hope to overthrowe his enemye. Againe, without [6] obedience,
neyther valiant man, ftout horfe, nor goodly harneffe, doth any good at all: which obedience of
the fouldiour toward the captaine, brought the hole
empyre of the world into the *Romaynes* handes, and,
when it was brought, kept it longer than ever it
was kept in any common wealthe before or after.
And this to be true, [7] *Scipio Africanus*, the moft
noble captaine that ever was among the *Romaynes*,
fhewed very plainly, what time as he went into
Africke to deftroy *Carthage*. For he refting his
hoaft by the way in *Sicilie*, a day or two, and at a
time ftandinge with a great man of *Sicilie*, and lokinge on his fouldiours how they exercifed themfelves

[3] Obedience. [4] Plat. leg. 12. [5] Xen. Agef. [6] Xen.
Hipp. [7] Plutarchus.

K   in

in kepinge of arraye, and other feates, the gentleman of *Sicilie* afked *Scipio*, wherein laye his chief
hope to overcome *Carthage?* He aunfwered, In
yonder fellowes of myne whom you fee playe:
And why? fayth the other; Becaufe fayth *Scipio*,
that, if I commanded them to runne into the top
of this high caftle, and caft themfelves downe backward upon thefe rockes, I am fure they would do
it. [8] *Saluft* alfo doth write, that there were mo
Romaynes put to death of their captaynes for fettinge on their enemyes before they had licence, than
were for runninge away out of the field, before
they had foughten. Thefe two examples do prove,
that amonges the *Romaynes*, the obedience of the
fouldiours was wonderfull greate, and the feveritye
of the captaynes, to fee the fame kept, wonderfull ftrayte. For they well perceived that an hoaft
full of obedience, falleth as feldome into the handes
of their enemyes, as that body falleth into jeopardye, the which is ruled by reafon. Reafon and
rulers being like in office, (for the one ruleth the
body of man, the other ruleth the body of the
common wealthe) oughte to be like of conditions,
and oughte to be obeyed in all manner of matters.
Obedience is nourifhed by feare and love, feare is

[8] Sal. in Cat.

kept

kept in by true juſtyce and equitye, love is gotten
by wyſedome, joyned by liberalitye. For where a
ſouldiour ſeeth righteouſneſſe ſo rule, that a man
can do neyther wronge, nor yet take wronge,
and that his captaine for his wyſedome can maintaine him, and for his liberalitye will maintaine
him, he muſt needes both love him and feare him,
of the which procedeth true and unfayned obedience.
After this inwarde vertue, the next good point in
a ſouldiour is to have and to handle his weapon
well, whereof the one muſt be at the appointment
of the captaine, the other lyeth in the courage and
exerciſe of the ſouldiour. Yet of all weapons, the
beſt is, as [9] *Euripides* doth ſaye, wherewith what
leaſt daunger of ourſelfe we may hurte our enemye
moſt. And that is (as I ſuppoſe) artillerie. Artillerie, now a dayes, is taken for two thinges:
gunnes and bowes, which, how much they do in
warre, both daily experience doth teache, and alſo
Peter Nannius, a learned man of *Louayn*, in a certaine dialogue doth very well ſet oute, wherein this is
moſt notable, that when he hath ſhewed excedinge
commodities of both, and ſome diſcommodities of
gunnes, as infinite coſt and charge, comberſome
carriage, and, if they be greate, the uncertaine

[9] In Herc. fur.

levelinge,

levelinge, the perill of them that ſtand by them,
the eaſyer avoidinge by them that ſtande farre of :
and, if they be litle, the leſſe both fear and jeo-
perdye is in them, beſyde all contrarye wether and
winde, which hindereth them not a litle; yet of all
ſhootinge he cannot reherſe one diſcommoditye.
PHI. That I marveile greatly at, ſeinge *Nannius* is
ſo well learned, and ſo exerciſed in the authors of
both the tongues : for I myſelfe do remember, that
ſhootinge in warre is but ſmallye prayſed, and that
of divers captaines in divers authors. For firſt in
Euripides, whom you ſo highlye prayſe (and verye
well, for *Tullye* thinketh everye verſe in him to be
an authoritye) what, I praye you, doth *Lycus*, that
overcame *Thebes*, ſaye as concerninge ſhootinge ?
whoſe wordes, as farre as I remember, be theſe, or
not much unlike.

What prayſe hath he at all, which never durſt abyde,
The dint of a ſpeares point thruſt againſt his ſyde.
Nor never bouldly buckeler bare yet in his left hande,
Face to face his enemies bront ſtiffelye to withſtande,
But alwaye truſteth to a bowe, and to a feathered ſticke,
Harneſſe ever moſt fit for him whiche to flie is quicke,
Bowe and ſhaft is armoure meteſt for a cowarde
Which dare not ones abide the bront of battaile ſharpe and harde.
But he a man of manhode moſt is mine aſſent,
Which, with hart and courage bould, fullie hath him bent,
His enemies loke in everye ſtoure ſtoutelie to abide,
Face to face, and foote to foote, tide what maye betide.

Eurip. in Herc. furent.

Againe,

Againe, *Teucer*, the beſt archer amonge all the *Grecians*, in [10] *Sophocles* is called of *Menelaus* a bowe-man, and a ſhooter, as in villianye aud reproach, to be a thinge of no price in warre. Moreover, *Pandarus*, the beſt ſhooter in the worlde, whom *Apollo* himſelfe taughte to ſhoote, both he and his ſhootinge is quite contemned in *Homer*, in ſo much that [1] *Homer* (which under a made fable doth alwayes hide his judgment of thinges) doth make *Pandarus* himſelfe crye out of ſhootinge, and caſt his bowe away, and take him to a ſpeare, makinge a vow, that if ever he came home, he would breake his ſhaftes, and burne his bowe, lamentinge greatlye, that he was ſo fonde to leave at home his horſe and chariot, with other weapons, for the truſt that he had in his bowe. *Homer* ſignifying thereby, that men ſhould leave ſhootinge out of warre, and take them to other weapons more fitte and able for the ſame, and I trowe *Pandarus* wordes be much what after this ſort.

If chaunce ill lucke me hyther brought,
Ill fortune me that day befell,
When firſt my bowe from the pynne I raughte,
For Hectors ſake, the Greekes to quell,
  But if that God ſo for me ſhape
That home againe I maye ones come,

[10] Sophoc. in Sia. Flag. [1] Iliad 5.

Nor

Let me never enjoye that hap,
Nor ever twife looke on the fonne,
If bowe and fhaftes I do not burne,
Which now fo evill doth ferve my turne.

But to let paſſe all poetes, what can be forer fayd
againſt any thinge, than the judgement of *Cyrus* is
againſt ſhootinge, which doth cauſe his *Perſians*,
being the beſt ſhooters, to lay away their [2] bowes,
and take them to ſwordes and bucklers, ſpeares and
dartes, and other like hande weapons. The which
thing *Zenophon*, ſo wyſe a philoſopher, ſo expert
a captaine in warre himſelfe, would never have
written, and ſpeciallye in that booke wherein he
purpoſed to ſhewe, as [3] *Tullye* ſayth indeede, not
the true hiſtorye, but the example of a perfite wyſe
Prince and common wealth, excepte that judgement of chaunging artillery into other weapons he
had alwayes thought beſt to be folowed in all warre.
Whoſe counſayle the [4] *Parthians* did folowe, when
they chaſed *Antonye* over the mountaynes of *Media*,
which beinge the beſt ſhooters of the worlde, lefte
theyr bowes, and toke them to ſpeares and moriſ-
pikes. And theſe fewe examples, I trowe, of the
beſte ſhooters, do well prove that the beſt ſhootinge
is not the beſt thing, as you call it, in warre. Tox.

[2] Xen. Cyr. Inſt. 6. [3] Epiſt. 1. ad Q. Fra. [4] Plutarch. M. Ant.

As

As concerninge your firſt example, taken out of
Euripides, I marveile you will bringe it for the diſ-
prayſe of ſhootinge, ſeeinge *Euripides* doth make
thoſe verſes, not becauſe he thinketh them true,
but becauſe he thinketh them fit for the perſon that
ſpake them. For indede his true judgement of
ſhootinge, he doth expreſſe by and by after in the
oration of the noble Captaine *Amphytrio* againſt *Lycus*, wherein a man maye doubte, whether he hath
more eloquentlye confuted *Lycus* ſayinge, or more
worthilye ſet oute the prayſe of ſhootinge. And as
I am adviſed, his wordes be much hereafter as I
ſhall ſaye.

Againſt the wittie gift of ſhootinge in a bowe,
Fonde and leude wordes thou leudlie doeſt out throwe,
Which if thou wilte heare of me a worde or twayne
Quicklie thou mayſt learne how fondlie thou doeſt blame.
  Firſt he that with his harneis himſelfe doth wall about,
That ſcarce is left one hole through which he may pepe out.
Such bond men to their harneis to fight are nothinge mete,
But ſoneſt of all other are troden under fete.
If he be ſtronge, his felowes faint, in whom he putteth his truſt,
So loded with his harneis he muſt nedes lie in the duſt,
Nor yet from death he cannot ſtart, if ones his weapon breke,
Howe ſtout, howe ſtronge, howe great, howe longe, ſo ever be ſuch a freke.
  But whoſoever can handle a bowe, ſturdie, ſtiffe, and ſtronge,
Wherewith like hayle manie ſhaftes he ſhootes into the thickeſt thronge :
This profite he takes, that ſtandinge a farre his enemies he may ſpill,
When he and his full ſafe ſhall ſtande, out of all daunger and ill.
And this in warre is wyſedome moſt, which workes our enemies woo,
When we ſhall be far from all ſeare and jeoperdie of our foo.

Eurip. in Herc. fur.

Secondarily,

Secondarily, even as I do not greatly regarde what *Menelaus* doth saye in *Sophocles* to *Teucer*, becaufe he fpake it both in anger, and alfo to him that he hated; even fo do I remember very well in *Homer*, that when *Hector* and the *Troyans* would have fet fyre on the *Greeke* fhips, *Teucer*, with his bowe, made them recule back againe, when *Menelaus* toke him to his feete, and ranne awaye.

Thirdlye, as concerninge *Pandarus*, [5] *Homer* doth not difprayfe the noble gift of fhootinge, but thereby everye man is taughte, that whatfoever, and howe good foever a weapon a man doth ufe in warre, if he be himfelfe a covetous wretche, a foole without counfaile, a peace breaker, as *Pandarus* was, at laft he fhall, throughe the punifhment of God, faule into his enemies bandes, as *Pandarus* did, whom *Diomedes*, throughe the helpe of *Minerva*, miferablye flue.

And, becaufe you make mention of *Homer*, and *Troye* matters, what can be more prayfe for any thinge, I praye you, than that is for fhootinge, that *Troye* could never be deftroyed without the help of *Hercules* fhaftes, which thing doth fignifye, that,

[5] Hom. Il, 5.

although

although all the world were gathered in an armye together, yet, without shootinge, they can never come
to their purpose, as *Ulysses*, in *Sophocles*, very plainlye
doth saye unto *Pyrrhus*, as concerning *Herçules*
shaftes to be carried into *Troye*.

Nor you without them, nor without you they do ought.   Soph. Phil.

Fourthlye, whereas *Cyrus* did chaunge part of
his bowmen, whereof he had plenty, in other men
of warre, whereof he lacked, I will not greatlye
dispute whether *Cyrus* did well in that pointe in
those dayes or no, becaufe it is plaine in [6] *Zenophon* howe stronge shooters the *Persians* were, what
bowes they had, what shaftes and heades they occupyed, what kind of warre theyr enemyes used.

But trulye, as for the *Parthians*, it is plaine in
[7] *Plutarche*, that, in chaunginge theyr bowes into
speares, they broughte theyr selfe into utter destruction. For when they had chafed the *Romaynes*
many a myle, throughe reafon of their bowes, at
the last the *Romaynes*, ashamed of their flyinge, and
remembringe theyr old noblenesse and courage,
imagined this way, that they would kneele down
on theyr knees, and so cover all theyr body with

[6] Xen. Cyri, Instit. 6. [7] Plut. in M. Anton.

L   theyr

theyr fhieldes and targettes, that the *Parthians* fhaftes might flide over them, and do them no harme; which thing when the *Parthians* perceyved, thinkinge that the *Romaynes* were forweryed with laboure, watche, and hunger, they layed downe theyr bowes, and toke fperes in theyr handes, and fo ranne upon them; but the *Romaynes* perceyving them without theyr bowes, rofe up manfullye, and flue them every mothers fonne, fave a fewe that faved themfelves with runninge awaye. And herein our archers of *Englande* farre paffe the *Parthians*, which for fuch a purpofe, when they fhall come to hand ftrokes, hath ever redye, eyther at his back hanginge, or els in his next felowes hand, a leaden maule, or fuch like weapon, to beat downe his enemies withall. PHI. Well, *Toxophile*, feeinge that thofe examples, which I had thought to have been cleane againft fhootinge, you have thus turned to the high prayfe of fhootinge: and all this prayfe that you have nowe fayde on it, is rather come in by me than fought for of you: let me heare, I praye you now, thofe examples which you have marked of fhootinge yourfelfe: whereby you are perfuaded, and thincke to perfwade other, that fhootinge is fo good in warre. TOX. Examples furely I have marked very manye; from the beginninge of time
                                                                had

had in memorye of writinge, throughout all common wealthes and empyres of the worlde : whereof the moſt parte I will paſſe over, leſt I ſhould be tedious : yet ſome I will touche, becauſe they be notable, both for me to tell and you to heare.

And becauſe the ſtorye of the *Jewes* is for the time moſt auncient, for the truthe moſt credible, it ſhall be moſt fitte to begin with them.   And althoughe I know that God is the onlye giver of victorye, and not the weapons, for all ſtrengthe and victorye (ſayth [8] *Judas Machabeus*) commeth from heaven : yet ſurelye ſtrong weapons be the inſtrumentes wherewith God doth overcome that parte, which he will have overthrown.   For God is well pleaſed with wyſe and witty feates of warre : as in meting of enemyes for truſe takinge, to have privilye in * a buſhmente harneſt men layed for feare of treaſon, as [9] *Judas Machabeus* did with *Nicanor*, *Demetrius* captaine.   And to have engines of warre to beat down cities withal : and to have ſcout watch amonges our enemyes to know theyr counſayles, as the noble captaine [10] *Jonathan*, brother to Ju-

[8] Mach. 1. 3.   [9] Mach. 2. 14.   [10] Mach. 1. 12.

* A buſhment] This word we do not remember elſewhere : perhaps it ſhould be in ambuſhment.

das

das Machabeus, did in the countrye of *Amathie,* againſt the mightye hoaſt of *Demetrius.* And, be-ſide all this, God is pleaſed to have goodlye tombes for them which do noble feates in warre, and to have theyr images made, and alſo theyr cote armours to be ſet above theyr tombes, to theyr perpetual laude and memorye! As the valiante captaine *Symon* did cauſe to be made for his brethren [1] *Judas Machabeus* and *Jonathan,* when they were ſlaine of the *Gentiles.* And thus, of what authoritye feates of warre, and ſtronge weapons be, ſhortlye and plainlye we may learne. But amonges the *Jewes,* as I begin to tell, I am ſure there was nothinge ſo occupyed, or did ſo much good as bowes did ; in ſo much, that when the *Jewes* had any great up-per-hand over the *Gentiles,* the firſt thinge alwayes that the captaine did, was to exhorte the people to geve all the thankes to God for the victorye, and not to theyr bowes, wherewith they had ſlaine theyr enemies : as it is plaine the noble [2] *Josue* did after ſo manye kinges thruſt downe by him.

God, when he promiſeth helpe to the *Jewes,* he uſeth no kind of ſpeakinge ſo much as this, that he will bende his bowe, and die his ſhaftes in the

[1] Mach. i. 13. [2] Joſ. 13.

Gentiles

[3] *Gentiles* bloud: whereby it is manifeſt, that eyther God will make the *Jewes* ſhoote ſtronge ſhootes to overthrowe theyr enemyes, or, at leaſt, that ſhootinge is a wonderfull mighty thinge in warre, whereunto the high power of God is likened. *David*, in the [4] *Pſalmes*, calleth bowes the veſſels of death, a bitter thinge, and, in an other place, a mightye power, and other wayes mo, which I will let paſſe, becauſe every man readeth them daily: but yet one place of Scripture I muſt needes remember, which is more notable for the prayſe of ſhootinge, than any that ever I redde in any other ſtorye, and that is, when [5] *Saule* was ſlaine by the *Philiſtines*, beinge mightye bowmen, and *Jonathan* his ſonne with him, that was ſo good a ſhooter, as the ſcripture ſayth, that he never ſhote ſhafte in vaine, and that the kingdome, after *Saules* death, came unto *David:* the firſt ſtatute and lawe that ever [6] *David* made after he was Kinge, was this, that all the children of *Iſraell* ſhould learne to ſhoote, according to a lawe made many a daye before that time, for the ſetting out of ſhootinge, as it is written (ſayth Scripture) in *Libro Juſtorum*, which booke we have not nowe. And thus we ſee

[3] Deut. 32. [4] Pſal. 7. 63. 75. [5] Regum 1. 31.
[6] Regum 2. 1.

plainly

plainly what great ufe of fhootinge, and what provifion even from the beginninge of the worlde for
fhootinge was amonge the *Jewes*.

The *Ethiopians* which inhabite the furtheft parte
South in the worlde, were wonderfull bowmen:
infomuch that when *Cambyfes* King of *Perfie*, being
in *Egypt*, fent certaine embaffadours into *Ethiope*
to the King there, with manye great giftes: the
King of [7] *Ethiope*, perceyvinge them to be efpyes,
toke them uppe fharpelye, and blamed *Cambyfes*
greatly for fuch unjuft enterprifes: but after that
he had princelye entertayned them, he fent for a
bowe, and bente it and drewe it, and then unbent
it againe, and fayd unto the embaffadours, you
fhall commende me to *Cambyfes*, and geve him this
bowe from me, and bidde him when any *Perfian*
can fhoote in this bowe, let him fet upon the *Ethiopians*: in the mean while let him geve thanckes
unto God, which doth not put in the *Ethiopians*
mindes to conquere any other mans lande.

This bowe, when it came amonge the *Perfians*,
never one man in fuch an infinite hoaft (as *Herodotus* doth faye) could ftyre the ftringe, fave only

[7] Herodotus in Thalia.

Smerdis,

Smerdis, the brother of *Cambyses*, which ftyred it two fingers, and no further: for the which acte *Cambyses* had such envye at him, that he afterwarde flue him: as doth appeare in the ftorye.

Sefoftris, the moft mightye Kinge that ever was in *Egypte*, overcame a great part of the world, and that by archers: he fubdued the *Arabians*, the *Jewes*, the *Affyrians*: he went farther in *Scythia* than anye man els: he overcame *Thracia*, even to the borders of *Germanye*. And, in token how he overcame all men, he fet uppe in manye places great images to his owne likeneffe, [8] havinge in one hand a bowe, in the other a fharpe headed fhafte: that men might knowe what weapon his hoaft ufed, in conqueringe fo manye people.

Cyrus, counted a God amonge the *Gentiles*, for his nobleneffe and felicitye in warre: yet, at the laft, when he fet upon the *Maffagetes*, [9] (which people never went without theyr bowe nor theyr quiver, neyther in warre nor peace) he and all his were flaine, and that by fhootinge, as appeareth in the ftorye.

[8] Herod. in Enterpe. Diod. Sic. 2. [9] Herod. in Clio.

Polycrates,

[10] *Polycrates*, the Prince of *Samos*, (a very litle
iſle) was lord over all the *Greeke* ſeas, and with-
ſtode the power of the *Perſians*, only by the helpe
of a thouſande archers.

The people of *Scythia*, of all other men, loved
and uſed moſt ſhootinge; the hole riches and
houſholde ſtuffe of a man in *Scythia* was a yoake
of oxen, a ploughe, his nagge and his dogge, his
bowe and his quiver: which quiver was covered
with the ſkin of a man, which he toke or ſlue firſt
in battaile. The *Scythians* to be invincible, by
reaſon of theyr ſhootinge, the great voyages of ſo
manye conquerours ſpente in that countrye in
vaine, doth well prove: but ſpeciallye that of *Da-*
rius the mightye King of *Perſia*, which, when he
had tarryed there a great ſpace, and done no good,
but had forwearyed his hoaſt with travaile and
hunger; at laſt the men of *Scythia* ſent an embaſ-
ſadour with four giftes, [1] a byrde, a frogge, a
mouſe and five ſhaftes. *Darius* marveylinge at the
ſtraungeneſſe of the giftes, aſked the meſſenger
what they ſignified: the meſſenger aunſwered, that
he had no further commandment, but only to de-
liver his giftes, and returne againe with all ſpede:

[10] Herod. in Thal.   [1] Herod. in Melpom.

But

But I am sure (sayth he) you *Persians* for your great wysedome can soone boult out what they meane. When the messenger was gone, every man began to say his verdite. *Darius* judgemente was this, that the *Scythians* gave over into the *Persians* handes theyr lives, theyr hole power, both by lande and sea, signifyinge by the mouse the earth, by the frogge the water, in which they both live, by the byrde theyr lives, which live in the ayre, by the shaft theyr hole power and empyre, that was maintayned always by shootinge. *Gobryas*, a noble and wyse captaine amonges the *Persians*, was of a clean contrarye minde, sayinge, Naye, not so, but the *Scythians* meane thus by theyr giftes, that excepte we gette us winges, and flye into the ayre like byrdes, or runne into the holes of the earth like myse, or els lye lurkinge in fennes and marishes, like frogges, we shall never returne home againe, before we be utterlye undone with theyr shaftes : which sentence sanke so sore into theyr hartes, that *Darius*, with all speede possible, brake uppe his campe and gat himselfe homewarde. Yet how much the *Persians* themselves sette by shootinge, whereby they encreased their empyre so much, doth appear by three manifest reasons: first that they brought uppe theyr youth in the schole

M   of

of fhootinge unto twentye years of age, as divers noble [2] *Greeke* authours do faye.

Againe, becaufe the noble Kinge [3] *Darius* thought himfelfe to be prayfed by nothinge fo much as to be counted a good fhooter, as doth appear by his fepulchre, wherein he caufed .to be written this fentence:

> Darius the King lyeth buried here,
> That in fhootinge and rydinge had never pere.
>
> Strab. 15.

Thirdlye, the [4] coyne of the *Perfians*, both golde and filver, had the armes of *Perfia* upon it, as is cuftomably ufed in other realmes, and that was bowe and arrowes: by the which feate they declared how much they fet by them.

The [5] *Grecians* alfo, but fpeciallye the noble *Athenienfes*, had all theyr ftrengthe lyinge in artillerie: and, for that purpofe, the citye of *Athens* had a thoufand men, which were only archers, in dailye wages, to watch and kepe the citye from all jeopardy and fodaine daunger: which archers alfo fhould carye to prifon and warde anye mifdoer, at

---

[2] Herod. in Clio. [3] Xen. in Cyr. Strab. 11. [4] Plutarch. in Angefila. [5] Suidas.

the

the commaundment of the highe officers, as plainlye doth appeare in [6] *Plato.* And surelye the bowmen of *Athens* did wonderfull feates in many bat-
tels, but speciallye when *Demosthenes*, the valiant
captaine, slue and toke prisoners all the *Lacedemonians*, besyde the citye of *Pylos*, where *Nestor* some
time was lorde: the shaftes went so thicke that day,
(sayth [7] *Thucidydes*) that no man could see theyr
enemyes. A *Lacedemonian*, taken prisoner, was
asked of one at *Athens*, whether they were stoute
fellowes that were slaine or no, of the *Lacedemonians?* He answered nothinge els but this: Make
much of those shaftes of youres, for they know
neyther stoute nor unstoute: meaninge thereby
that no man (though he were never so stoute) came
in theyr walke that escaped without death.

[8] *Herodotus* descrybinge the mightye hoast of
Xerxes, especiallye doth marke oute, what bowes
and shaftes they used, signifyinge that therein laye
theyr chiefe strengthe. And at the same time
Atossa, mother of *Xerxes*, wyfe to *Darius*, and
daughter of *Cyrus*, doth enquire, (as [9] *Aeschylus*
sheweth in a tragedye) of a certaine messenger that

[6] Plato in Protagora. [7] Thucydid. 4. [8] Herod. in Polym. [9] Æsch. in Perf.

M 2   came

came from *Xerxes* hoaſt, what ſtronge and fearfull
bowes the *Grecians* uſed : whereby it is playne, that
artillerye was the thinge, wherein both *Europe* and
Aſia in thoſe days truſted moſt upon.

The beſt part of *Alexanders* hoaſt were archers,
as plainlye doth appeare by *Arrianus*, and other
that wrote his life : and thoſe ſo ſtrong archers, that
they onlye, ſundry times overcame theyr enemyes
afore any other needed to fighte : as was ſeene in
the battaile which *Nearchus*, one of *Alexanders* captaines, had beſyde the ryver *Thomeron*. And therefore, as concerninge all theſe kingdomes and common wealthes, I maye conclude with this ſentence
of [10] *Plinye*, whoſe wordes be, as I ſuppoſe, thus :
" If anye man would remember the *Ethiopians*,
" *Egyptians*, *Arabians*, the men of *Inde*, of *Scythia*,
" ſo many people in the Eaſte of the *Sarmatianes*,
" and all the kingdomes of the *Parthians*, he ſhall
" perceive halfe the parte of the worlde to live in
" ſubjection, overcome by the mighte and power
" of ſhootinge."

In the common wealth of *Rome*, which exceeded
all other in vertue, nobleneſſe and dominion, little

[10] Plin. lib. 16. cap. 36.

mention

mention is made of fhootinge, not becaufe it was
little ufed amonges them, but rather becaufe it was
fo neceffarye and common, that it was thought a
thinge not neceffarye or required of anye man to
be fpoken upon ; as if a man fhould defcrybe a
great feaft, he would not ones name breade, althoughe it be moft common and neceffarye of all:
but furelye, if a feaft, being never fo great, lacked
breade, or had fewftye and noughtye breade, all
the other daintyes fhould be unfaverye, and litle
regarded, and then would men talke of the com-
modutye of bread, when they lacke it, that would
not ones name it afore, when they had it : and
even fo did the *Romaynes*, as concerninge fhootinge.
Seldome is fhootinge named, and yet it did the
moft good in warre, as did appeare verye plainlye
in that battaile, which *Scipio Africanus* had with
the *Numantines* in *Spaine*, whom he could never
overcome, before he fet bowemen amonges his horfe-
men, by whofe might they were cleane vanquifhed.

Againe, [1] *Tiberius*, fightinge with *Armenius* and
Inquiomerus, Princes of *Germayne*, had one winge
of archers on horfebacke, an other of archers on
foote, by whofe might the *Germaynes* were flaine

[1] Cor. Tac. 2.

downright,

downright, and fo fcattered and beate out of the
fielde, that the chafe lafted ten miles; the *Germaynes* clame up into trees for feare, but the *Romaynes*
did fetche them downe with theyr fhaftes, as they
had been birdes, in which battaile the *Romaynes* loft
few or none, as doth appeare in the hiftorye.

But as I beganne to faye, the *Romaynes* did not
fo much prayfe the goodneffe of fhootinge, when
they had it, as they did lament the lacke of it, when
they wanted it, as *Leo* the V. the noble Emperour,
dothe plainly teftifye in fundrye places in thofe
bookes which he wrote in *Greeke, of the fleightes and
pollicies of warre.* PHI. Surelye of that booke
I have not heard before, and how came you to the
fight of it. TOX. The booke is rare ttulye,
but this laft yeare, when Maifter *Cheke* tranflated
the fayde booke oute of *Greeke* into *Latine*, to the
Kings Majeftye, *Henrye* the Eyght, of noble memorye, he, of his gentleneffe, would have me verye
oft in his chamber, and, for the familiaritye that
I had with him, more than manye other, would
fuffer me to reade of it, when I would, the which
thinge to do, furelye I was verye defirous and glad,
becaufe of the excellent handelinge of all thinges,
that ever he taketh in hande. And verilye, *Phi-
loge,*

lologe, as oft as I remember the departinge of that
[2] man from the *Univerſitye*, (which thinge I do not
feldome) ſo ofte do I well perceive our moſt helpe
and furtheraunce to learninge, to have gone away
with him. For, by the great commoditye that we
toke in hearinge him reade privately in his chamber,
all *Homer*, *Sophocles*, and *Euripides*, *Herodotus*, *Thu-
cydides*, *Zenophon*, *Iſocrates*, and *Plato*, we feele the
great diſcommodity in not hearinge of him, *Ariſtotle* and *Demoſthenes*, which two authours, with all
diligence, laſt of all, he thought to have redde unto
us. And when I conſider howe manye men be
ſuccoured with his helpe, and his ayde to abyde
here for learninge, and howe all men were provoked and ſtyrred up, by his counſayle and dailye
example, howe they ſhould come to learninge,
ſurelye I perceive that ſentence of *Plato* to be true,
which ſayeth : " that there is nothinge better in
" anye common wealthe, than that there ſhould
" be alwayes one or other excellent paſſinge man,
" whoſe life and vertue ſhoulde plucke forwarde
" the will, diligence, laboure, and hope of all
" other, that, folowinge his foot-ſteppes, they
" might come to the ſame ende, whereunto labour,
" learninge and vertue, had conveyed him before."

[2] Sir John Cheke.

The

The great hinderaunce of learninge, in lackinge this man, greatly I fhould lament, if this difcommoditye of ours were not joyned with the commoditye and wealth of the whole realme, for which purpofe our noble Kinge, full of wyfedome, called uppe this excellent man, full of learninge, to teache noble Prince *Edwarde*, an office full of hope, comforte, and folace, to all true hartes of *Englande*: for whom all *Englande* dailye doth praye, that he, paffing his tutour in learninge and knowledge, followinge his father in wyfedome and felicitye, accordinge to that example which is fet afore his eyes, maye fo fet oute and maintayne Gods word, to the abolifhment of all papiftry, the confufion of all herefye, that thereby be feared of his enemyes, loved of all his fubjects, may bring to his own glorye immortal fame and memory, to this realme, wealth, honour, and felicity, to true and unfained religion perpetuall peace, concord and unitye.

But to returne to fhootinge againe, what *Leo* fayth of fhootinge, amonges the *Romaynes*, his wordes be fo much for the prayfe of fhootinge, and the booke alfo fo rare to be gotten, that I learned the places by hearte, which be, as I fuppofe, even this. Firft in his fixte book, as concerninge what
harneffe

harneſſe is beſt : [3] " Let all the youth of *Rome* be
" compelled to uſe ſhootinge, eyther more or leſs,
" and alwayes to beare theyr bowe and theyr quiver
" aboute with them, untill they be eleven yeares
" olde." For ſithens ſhootinge was neglected and
decayed amonge the *Romaynes*, many a battayle and
fielde hath bene loſt. Agayne, in the eleventh
booke and fiftieth chapter, (I call that by bookes
and chapters, which the *Greeke* book divideth by
chapters and paragraphes) [4] " Let your ſouldiours
" have theyr weapons well appointed and trimmed,
" but, above all other thinges, regard moſt ſhoot-
" inge, and therefore let men, when there is no
" warre, uſe ſhootinge at home. For the leavinge
" off onelye of ſhootinge, hath brought in ruine
" and decaye the whole empyre of *Rome*."

Afterwarde he commaundeth agayne his captaine
by theſe wordes. [5] " Arme your hoaſte as I have
" appointed you, but eſpeciallye with bowe and
" arrowes plentye. For ſhootinge is a thing of
" much mighte and power in warre, and chieflye
" agaynſt the *Saracenes* and *Turkes*, which people
" hath all theyr hope of victorye in theyr bowe

[3] Leo. 6. 5. [4] Leo. 11. 50. [5] Leo. 18. 21.

N   " and

" and ſhaftes." Beſides all this, in an other place,
he wryteth thus to his captayne. [6] " Artillerye is
" eaſy to be prepared, and, in time of great nede,
" a thinge moſt profitable, therefore we ſtraitelye
" commaund you to make proclamation to all men
" under our dominion, which be eyther in warre
" or peace, to all cities, borrowes, and townes, and
" finally, to all maner of men, that every ſere per-
" ſon have bowe and ſhaftes of his owne, and
" everye houſe beſides this to have a ſtandinge
" bearinge bowe, and forty ſhaftes for all nedes,
" and that they exerciſe themſelves in holts, hilles,
" and dales, plaines and woods, for all maner of
" chaunces in warre."

How much ſhootinge was uſed among the olde
Romaynes, and what meanes noble captaynes and
emperours made to have it increaſe amonges them,
and what hurte came by the decaye of it, theſe
wordes of *Leo* the Emperour, which, in a maner, I
have rehearſed word for word, plainly doth declare.

And yet ſhootinge, althoughe they ſet never ſo
much by it, was never ſo good then, as it is now
in *Englande*; which thinge to be true is very pro-

[6] Leo. 20. 79.

bable,

bable, in that *Leo* doth fay, [7] " Thát he would " have his fouldiours take off theyr arrow heades, " and one fhoote at another, for theyr exercife;" which play if *Englifh* archers ufed, I thincke they fhould finde fmall playe, and leffe pleafure in it at all.

The greate upperhande maintayned alwayes in warre by artillerye, doth appear very plainlye by this reafon alfo, that when the *Spaniardes*, *French-men*, and *Germaynes*, *Greekes*, *Macedonians*, and *Egyptians*, eche countrye ufinge one finguler wea-pon, for which they were greatlye feared in warre, as the *Spaniarde Lancea*, the *Frenchman Gefa*, the *Germane Framea*, the *Grecian Machera*, the *Mace-donian Sariffa*, yet could they not efcape but be fub-jectes to the empyre of *Rome*, when the *Parthians*, having all theyr hope in artillerye, gave no place to them, but overcame the [8] *Romaynes* ofter than the *Romaynes* them, and kept battel with them many an hundred yeare, and flue the riche *Craffus* and his fonne, with many a ftout *Romayne* more, with theyr bowes; they drave *Marcus Antonius* over the hills of *Media* and *Armenia*, to his great fhame and

[7] Leo. 7. 13.   [8] Plutarch. in Craff. & in M. Anton. Ael. Spart.

reproche;

reproche; they flue *Julianus Apoftata*, and *Anto-nius Caracalla*; they held in perpetuall prifon the moft noble Emperour *Valerian*, in defpyte of all the *Romaynes* and many other princes, which wrote for his deliveraunce, as *Belfolis*, called King of Kinges, *Valerius*, Kinge of *Cadufia*, *Arthabefdes*, King of *Armenia*, and manye other Princes more, whome the *Parthians*, by reafon of theyr artillerye, regarded never one whitte, and thus with the *Romaynes*, I maye conclude, that the borders of theyr empyre were not at the funne ryfinge and funne fettinge, as *Tullye* fayth; but fo farre they went, as artillerye would geve them leave. For, I thinck, all the ground that they had, eyther Northward, further than the borders of *Scythia*, or Eaftward, further than the borders of ⁹ *Parthia*, a man might have bought with a fmall deale of money, of which thinge furely fhootinge was the caufe.

From the fame country of *Scythia*, the *Gothians*, *Hunnes*, and *Vandalians*, came with the fame wea-pon of artillerye, as *Paulus Diaconus* doth faye, and fo bereft *Rome* of her empyre by fyre, fpoyle, and wafte, fo that in fuch a learned city was left fcarce one man behinde, that had learninge or leifure to

⁹ Paulus Dia.

leave

leave in writinge to them which fhould come after
how fo noble an empyre, in fo fhort a while, by a
rabble of banifhed bond-men, withoute all order
and pollicye, fave onely theyr naturall and dailye
exercyfe in [10] artillerye, was broughte to fuch
thraldome and ruine.

After them the *Turkes*, having another name
but yet the fame people, borne in *Scythia*, brought
uppe onely in artillerye, by the fame weapon have
fubdued and bereft from the *Chriften* men all *Afia*
and *Affricke* (to fpeak upon) and the moft noble
countryes of *Europe*, to the greate demynifhing of
Chriftes Religion, to the greate reproache of co-
wardyfe of all Chriftianitye, a manifeft token of Gods
high wrath and difpleafure over the finne of the
worlde, but fpeciallye amonges [1] Chriften men,
which be on flepe, made druncke with the fruites
of the flefh, as infidelitye, difobedience to Gods
word, and herefie, grudge, ill will, ftrife, open
battaile, and privy envye, covetoufneffe, oppreffion,
unmercifulneffe, with innumerable fortes of unfpeakable daily bawdrye : which thinges furelye, if
God holde not his holye hand over us, and plucke
us from them, will bringe us to a more *Turkifhnes*,

[10] P. Mela. [1] Nota.

and

and more beaſtelye blind barbarouſneſſe, as callinge
ill thinges good, and good thinges ill. Contemn-
ynge of knowledge and learninge, ſettinge at nought,
and having for a fable, God and his hyghe providence, will bringe us, I ſay, to a more ungracious
Turkiſhnes, if more *Turkiſhnes* can be than this, than
if the *Turkes* had ſworne to brynge all *Turkye* againſt
us. For theſe fruites ſurelye muſt needes ſprynge
of ſuch ſeede, and ſuch effect needes folow of ſuch
a cauſe, if reaſon, truth, and God be not altered,
but as they are wont to be. For ſurelye no *Turk-*
iſhe power can overthrow us, if *Turkiſhe* lyfe do not
caſte us downe before. If God were with us, it
buted not the *Turke* to be againſt us, but our un-
faythfull ſinneful livinge which is the *Turkes* mother, and hath brought him uppe hitherto, muſte
needes turne God from us, becauſe ſinne and he
hath no felowſhippe together. If we baniſhed ill
lyvinge oute of Chriſtendome, I am ſure the *Turke*
ſhould not onely not overcome us, but ſcarce have
an hole to runne into in his owne countrye.

But Chriſtendome now, I may tell you, *Philo-*
loge, is much like a man that hath an itch on him,
and lyeth dronke alſo in his bed, and though a
theefe come to the dore, and heaveth at it, to come

in

in and sleye him, yet he lyeth in his bedde, having more pleasure to lye in a slumber and scratch
himselfe where it itcheth, even to the harde bone,
than he hath redinesse to rise uppe lustely, and
drive him away that would robbe him and sleye
him.   But I trust, Christ will so lighten and lift
uppe Christen mens eyes, that they shall not sleepe
to death, nor that the *Turke*, Christs open enemy,
shall ever boast that he hath quite overthrown us.

But, as I began to tell you, shootinge is the
chyefe thinge wherewith God suffereth the *Turke*
to punishe our noughtye lyvinge withall : the
youth there is broughte uppe in shootinge, his
privy garde for his own persoune is bowmen, the
might of theyr shootinge is well knowen of the
[2] *Spanyardes*, which at the town called *Newecastle*,
in *Illyrica*, were quite slaine uppe, of the *Turkes*
arrowes : when the *Spanyardes* had no use of theyr
gunnes by reason of the raine.   And now, last of
all, the Emperours majestye himselfe, at the citye
of *Argier* in *Affricke*, had his hoast sore handled
with the *Turkes* arrowes, when his gunnes were
quite dispatched, and stode him in no service because of the raine that fell, whereas in such a

[2] Casp. de rebus Turc.

chaunce

chaunce of raine, if he had had bowmen, furely theyr fhotte mighte peradventure have bene a little hindered, but quite difpatched and marde it could never have bene. But, as for the *Turkes*, I am werye to talke of them, partlye becaufe I hate them, and partlye becaufe I am now affectioned even as it were a man that had bene longe wanderinge in ftraunge countries, and would fayne be at home to fee how well his own frendes profper and lead theyr lyfe. And furelye, me thincke, I am verye merye at my hart to remember how I fhall finde at home in *Englande*, amonges *Englifhmen*, partely by hiftoryes of them that have gone afore us, againe by experience of them which we knowe and live with us, as greate noble feates of warre by artil-lerye as ever was done at anye time in any other com-mon wealthe. And here I muft nedes remember a certaine *Frenchman*, called [3] *Textor*, that writeth a booke which he nameth *Officina*, wherein he weaveth up many broken ended matters, and fettes out much riffraffe, pelfery, trumpery, baggage, and beggery ware, clamparde up of one that would feeme to be fitter for a fhop indede than to wryte anye booke. And, amonges all other ill packed up matters, he thruftes uppe in a heepe together

[3] Textor.

all

all the good fhooters that ever hath bene in the
worlde, and he fayth himfelfe, and yet I trowe,
Philologe, that all the examples which I now, by
chaunce, have reherfed out of the beft authors
both in *Greke* and *Latine*, *Textor* hath but two of
them, which two furelye, if they were to reckon
againe, I would not ones name them, partlye becaufe they were noughtye perfons, and fhootinge
fo muche the worfe, becaufe they loved it, as *Domitian* and *Commodus*, the Emperours: partlye becaufe *Textor* hath them in his booke, on whom I
loked by chaunce in the booke-binders fhoppe,
thinckinge of no fuch matter. And one thinge I
will faye to you, *Philologe*, that if I were difpofed
to do it, and you had leyfure to hear it, I could
fone do as *Textor* doth, and reckon uppe fuch a
rabble of fhooters that be named here and there
in poetes, as would hold us talkinge whiles to-
morrow: but my purpofe was not to make mention of thofe which were fayned of poetes for theyr
pleafure, but of fuche as were proved in hiftoryes
for a truthe. But why I bringe in *Textor* was
this: at laft, when he hath rekened all fhooters
that he can, he fayth thus, 4 *Petrus Crinitus* wryteth, that the *Scottes*, which dwell beyonde *Eng-*

4 P. Crin. 3. 10.

O   *lande,*

lande, be very excellent shooters, and the best bowmen in warre. This sentence, whether *Crinitus*
wrote is more leudlye of ignorance, or *Textor* confirmeth it more pivishlye of envye, maye be called
in queftion and doubt, but this furelye do I knowe
verye well, that *Textor* hath both redde in *Gaguinus* the *Frenche* hiftorye, and alfo hath hearde his
father or graunde father talke (excepte per chaunce
he was born and bredde in a cloyfter) after that fort
of the fhootinge of *Englifhmen*, that *Textor* neded
not to have gone fo pivifhlye beyonde *Englande* for
fhootinge, but might very foon, even into the firft
towne of *Kent*, have found fuch plentye of fhootinge, as is not in all the realme of *Scotlande* againe.
The *Scottes* furelye be good men of warre in theyr
owne feates as can be: but as for fhootinge, they
neyther can ufe it for any profite, nor yet will
chalenge it for any praife, althoughe Maifter *Textor*,
of his gentleneffe, would geve it them. *Textor*
neded not to have filled up his booke with fuch
lyes, if he had redde the hiftorye of *Scotlande*, which
   5 *Johannes Major* doth wryte: wherein he might
have learned, that when *James Stewart*, firft Kinge
of that name, at the parliamente holden at *Saint
Johns* towne, or *Perthie*, commaundinge under

5 John Major 6.

paine

paine of great forfite, that everye *Scotte* fhould learne to fhoote: yet neyther the love of theyr countrye, the feare of theyr enemyes, the avoydinge of punifhment, nor the receyvinge of any profite that might come by it, could make them to be good archers: which be unapte and unfitte thereunto by Gods providence and nature.

Therefore the *Scottes* themfelves prove *Textor* a lyer, both with auctoritye and alfo daily experience, and by a certaine proverbe that they have amonges theyr communication, whereby they geve the whole prayfe of fhootinge honeftlye to *Englifh-men*, fayinge thus: that *Every Englifh archer beareth under his girdle twenty-four Scottes.*

But to let *Textor* and the *Scottes* go, yet one thinge would I wifhe for the [6] *Scottes*, and that is this, that feeinge one God, one fayth, one compaffe of the fea, one land and countrye, one tounge in fpeakinge, one maner and trade in lyvinge, like courage and ftomache in warre, like quickeneffe of witte to learninge, hath made *Englande* and *Scotlande* both one, they would fuffer them no longer to be

[6] John Major 6. Hift. Scot.

two:

two : but cleane geve over the *Pope*, which feeketh none other thinge (as manye a noble and wyfe *Scottifhe* man doth knowe) but to fede uppe diffention and parties betwixte them and us, procuringe that thinge to be two, which God, nature, and reafon would have one.

How profitable fuch an * attonemente were for *Scotlande*, both *Johannes Major* and *Hector Boetius*, which wrote the *Scottes* chronicles, do tell, and alfo all the gentlemen of *Scotlande*, with the poore communaltye, do well knowe : fo that there is nothinge that ftoppeth this matter, fave only a few fryers, and fuch like, which, with the dregges of our *Englifhe* Papiftrye lurkinge amonges them, ftudye nothing els but to brewe battaile and ftrife betwixt both the people : whereby onlye they hope to maintaine theyr papifticall kingdome, to the deftruction of the noble bloude of *Scotlande*, that then they maye with authoritye do that, which neyther noble man nor poor man in *Scotlande* yet doth know. And as for *Scottifhe* men and *Englifh* men be not ennemyes by nature, but by cuftome ; not by our good will, but by theyr own follye : which fhould take more honour in being copled to *Eng-*

* Attonement is Union, or the act of fetting at one.

lande,

lande, than we fhould take profite in beinge joyned
to *Scotlande.*

Wales beinge headye and rebelling many yeares
againſt us, laye wilde, untylled, uninhabited without lawe, juſtice, civilitye and order; and then
was amonges them more ſtealinge than true dealinge, more ſuretye for them that ſtudyed to be
nought, than quietneſſe for them that laboured to
be good: when nowe, thancked be God and noble
Englande, there is no countrye better inhabited,
more civile, more diligent in honeſt craftes, to get
both true and plentifull livinge withall. And this felicitye (my minde geveth me) fhould have chaunced
alſo to *Scotlande,* by the godlye wyſedome of the
moſt noble Prince Kinge *Henrye* the VIII. by whom
God wrought more wonderfull thinges than ever
by anye Prince before: as baniſhinge the biſhoppe
of *Rome* and hereſye, bringinge to light Gods word
and veritye, eſtabliſhinge ſuch juſtice and equitye
throughe everye part of this realme, as never was
ſeene afore.

But *Textor* (I beſhrowe him) hath almoſt brought
us from our communication of ſhootinge. Now
Sir, by my judgemente, the artillerye of *Englande*
farre

farre exceedeth all other realmes : but yet one
thinge I doubt, and long have furely in that point
doubted, when, or by whom, fhootinge was firft
brought into *Englande* ; and, for the fame purpofe,
as I was once in companye with Sir *Thomas Eliot*
knighte, which furely for his learninge in all kinde
of knowledge, brought muche worfhippe to all the
nobilitye of *Englande*, I was fo bould to afke him,
if he at any time had marked any thinge, as concerninge the bringinge in of fhootinge into *Eng-*
lande : he aunfwered me gentlye againe, he had a
worke in hand, which he nameth, *De rebus memo-*
rabilibus Angliæ, which I truft we fhall fee in print
fhortlye, and, for the accomplifhement of that
booke, he had redde and perufed over manye ould
monuments of *Englande*, and, in feeking for that
purpofe, he marked this of fhootinge in an excedinge olde chronicle, the which had no name, that
what time as the *Saxons* came firft into this realme,
in kinge *Vortigers* dayes, when they had bene here
a while, and at laft began to faule out with the
Britaynes, they troubled and fubdued the *Britaynes*
with nothinge fo much as with theyr bowe and
fhaftes, which weapon beinge ftraunge and not
feene here before, was wonderfull terrible unto
them, and this beginninge I can thincke verye well
to

to be true. But now as concerninge many examples for the prayſe of *Engliſhe* archers in warre,
ſurelye I will not be longe in a matter that no man
doubteth in, and thoſe fewe that I will name, ſhall
eyther be proved by the hiſtoryes of our enemyes,
or els done by men that now live.

King *Edwarde* the thirde, at the battaile of *Creſſie*,
againſt *Philip* the *French* King, as *Gaguinus*, the
French hiſtoriographer, plainlye doth tell, ſlewe
that daye all the nobilitye of *Fraunce* onlye with his
archers.

Such like battaile alſo fought the noble black
Prince *Edwarde* beſide *Poiƈters*, where *John* the
French Kinge, with his ſonne, and in a manner
all the peres of *Fraunce* were taken, beſides thirty
thouſand which that daye were ſlaine, and very few
Engliſhe men, by reaſon of theyr bowes.

Kinge *Henrye* the fifte, a Prince pereleſſe and
moſt victorious conquerour of all that ever dyed
yet in this parte of the worlde, at the battle of *Agin-
court*, with ſeven thouſand fightinge men, and yet
manye of them ſicke, being ſuche archers, as the
chronicle ſayth, that moſt parte of them drewe a
yarde,

yarde, flewe all the chevalrye of *Fraunce*, to the number of forty thoufand and mo, and loft not paft twenty-fix *Englifhmen*.

The bloudye civill warre of *Englande* betwixte the houfe of *Yorke* and *Lancafter*, where fhaftes flewe of both fydes to the deftruction of manye a yoman of *Englande*, whom foreine battell could never have fubdued, both I will paffe over for the pytifulneffe of it, and yet maye we highlye prayfe God in the remembraunce of it, feinge he, of his providence, hath fo knitte together thofe two noble houfes, with fo noble and pleafaunte a flowre.

The excellent Prince *Thomas Howarde* Duke of *Norfolke*, with bowemen of *Englande*, flewe Kinge *Jamye* with manye a noble *Scotte*, even brant againft *Floden* hill, in which battell the ftoute archers of *Chefhyre* and *Lancafhyre*, for one daye beftowed to the death for theyr Prince and countrye fake, hath gotten immortall name and prayfe for ever.

The feare onlye of *Englifhe* archers hath done more wonderfull thinges than ever I redde in anye hiftorye, *Greke* or *Latine*, and moft wonderfull of all now of late, befyde *Carlifle*, betwixt *Efke* and *Leven*,

Leven, at *Sandyesikes,* where the whole nobilitye of
Scotlande, for feare of the archers of *Englande,* (next
the ftroke of God) as both *Englifhe* and *Scottifhe*
men that were prefent hath tolde me, were drowned
and taken prifoners.

Nor that noble acte alfo, which althoughe it be
almoft loft by time, cometh not behinde in wor-
thineffe, which my fingular good frende and maifter
Sir William Walgrave and *Sir George Somerfet* did,
with a fewe archers, to the number, as it is fayd,
of fixteen, at the turnpike befyde *Hammes,* where
they turned with fo fewe archers fo manye *French-
men* to flight, and turned fo manye out of theyr
* jackes, which turne turned all *Fraunce* to fhame
and reproach; and thofe two noble knightes to
perpetuall prayfe and fame.

And thus you fee, *Philologe,* in all countryes,
Afia, Affricke, and *Europe,* in *Inde, Ethiop, Egypt,*
and *Jurie, Parthia, Perfia, Grece* and *Italye, Scythia, Turkye,* and *Englande,* from the beginninge
of the world even to this daye, that fhootinge hath
had the chiefe ftroke in warre. PHI. Thefe examples furelye apte for the prayfe of fhootinge, not

* A Jack is a coat of mail.

P   fayned

fayned by poetes, but proved by true hiftoryes, diftinct by time and order, hath delited me exceeding much, but yet methincke that all this prayfe belongeth to ftronge fhootinge and drawinge of mightye bowes, not to prickinge and nere fhootinge, for which caufe you and many other doth love and ufe fhootinge.   Tox. Evermore, *Philologe*, you will have fome overthwarte reafon to drawe forth more communication withal, but neverthelefle, you fhall perceyve if you will, that ufe of prickinge, and defire of nere fhootinge at home, are the onlye caufes of ftronge fhootinge in warre, and why? For you fee that the ftronge men do not draw alwayes the ftrongeft fhote, which thinge proveth that drawinge ftronge lyeth not fo much in the ftrengthe of man, as in the ufe of fhootinge. And experience teacheth the fame in other thinges, for you fhall fee a weake fmithe, which will with a lipe and turninge of his arme, take uppe a barre of yron, that another man, thrife as ftronge, cannot ftirre.   And a ftronge man not ufed to fhoote, hath his armes, breaft and fhoulders, and other parts wherewith he fhould drawe ftronglye, one hinderinge and ftoppinge another, even as a dozen ftronge horfes not ufed to the cart, lettes and troubles one another.   And fo the more ftronge

man

man not ufed to fhoote, fhootes moft unhanfum-
lye, but yet if a ftrong man with ufe of fhooting
coulde apply all the partes of his bodye together, to
theyr mofte ftrength, then fhould he both drawe
ftronger than other, and alfo fhoote better than
other. But nowe a ftronge man not ufed to fhoote,
at a girde, can heve up and plucke in funder many
a good bowe, as wilde horfes at a brunt doth race
and plucke in pieces many a ftronge carte. And
thus ftronge men, without ufe, can do nothinge
in fhootinge to any purpofe, neyther in warre nor
peace, but if they happen to fhoote, yet they have
done within a fhote or two, when a weake man
that is ufed to fhoote, fhall ferve for all times and
purpofes, and fhall fhoote ten fhaftes againft the
others four, and drawe them uppe to the pointe
every time, and fhoote them to the moft advantage,
drawinge and withdrawinge his fhafte when he lift,
marking at one man, yet letdryvinge at an other
man: which thinges, in a fet battaile, althoughe
a man fhall not always ufe, yet in bickeringes, and
at overthwart meetinges, when few archers be together, they do moft good of all.

Againe, he that is not ufed to fhoote, fhall evermore with untowardneffe of houldinge his bowe,

and

and nockinge his fhafte, not lokinge to his ftringe betime, put his bowe alwayes in jeopardye of break-inge, and then he were better to be at home, more-over he fhall fhoote very few fhaftes, and thofe full unhandfumly, fome not halfe drawen, fome to high and fome to low, nor he cannot drive a fhote at a time, nor ftoppe a fhote at a nede, but out muft it, and very oft to evill profe.

Phi. And that is beft, I trowe, in warre, to let it go, and not to ftoppe it.　　Tox. No not fo, but fome time to hould a fhaft at the head, which if they be but few archers, doth more good with the fear of it, than it fhould do if it were fhotte with the ftroke of it.　　Phi. That is a wonder to me, that the fear of a difpleafure-fhould do more harme than the difpleafure itfelfe.　　Tox. Yes, ye knowe that a man which feareth to be banifhed oute of his countrye, can neyther be merye, eate, drincke, nor fleepe for feare; yet when he is ba-nifhed in dede, he fleepeth and eateth as well as any other.　　And many men, doubtinge and fear-inge whether they fhould dye or no, even for very fear of death, preventeth themfelfe with a more bit-ter death, than the other death fhould have bene indede.　　And thus fear is worfe than the thing

feared,

feared, as is pretelye proved by the communication
of [7] *Cyrus* and *Tigranes*, the Kinges sonne of *Ar-
menie*, in *Zenophon*.

PHI. I graunt, *Toxophile*, that ufe of fhootinge
maketh a man drawe stronge, to fhoote at most advantage, to kepe his gere, which is no fmall thinge
in warre; but yet methincke that the customable
fhootinge at home, fpeciallye at buttes and prickes,
make nothinge at all for stronge fhootinge, which
doth most good in warre. Therefore, I fuppofe,
if men fhould ufe to go into the fieldes, and learne
to fhoote mightye stronge fhotes, and never care
for anye mark at all, they fhould do much better.
Tox. The truthe is, that fafhion much ufed would
do much good, but this is to be feared, least that
waye could not provoke men to ufe much fhootinge, becaufe there fhould be litle pleafure in it.
And that in fhooting is beste, that provoketh a man
to ufe fhooting most: for much ufe maketh men
fhoote both stronge and well, which two thinges
in fhooting every man doth defyre. And the chiefe
maintayner of ufe in anye thinge is comparifon and
honest contention. For when a man stryveth to be
better than an other, he will gladlye ufe that thinge,

[7] Cyroped. 3.

though

though it be never so painful, wherein he would excell, which thinge *Aristotle* very pretelye doth note, sayinge, [8] " Where is comparison, there is victorye; " where is victorye there is pleasure : and where " is pleasure, no man careth what labour or paine " he taketh, because of the prayse and pleasure that " he shall have in doing better than other men."

Agayne, you knowe, *Hesiodus*, writeth to his brother *Perses*, [9] " that all craftesmen, by contend- " inge one honestlye with another, do encrease " theyr cunninge with theyr substance." And therefore in *London*, and other great cityes, men of one crafte, most commonlye, dwell together, because in honest strivinge together, who shall do best, everye one maye waxe both cunninger and rycher. So likewyse in shootinge, to make matches to assemble archers together, to contend who shall shoote best, and winne the game, en- creaseth the use of shootinge wonderfullye amonges men. PHI. Of use you speake verye muche, *Toxophile*, but I am sure in all other matters use can do nothinge, withoute two other thinges be joyned with it, one is a naturall aptnesse to a thinge, the other is a true waye or knowledge, howe to do

[8] Arist. Rhet. [9] Hesiod. in Op. et die.

the

the thinge, to which two if ufe be joyned as thirde felowe of them three, procedeth perfectneffe and excellencye : if a man lacke the firft two, aptneffe and cunninge, ufe can do litle good at all.

For he that would be an oratour, and is nothinge naturallye fitte for it, that is to faye, lacketh a good witte and memorye, lacketh a good voyce, countenaunce and bodye, and other fuch like, yea, if he had all thefe, and knowe not what, howe, where, when, nor to whom he fhoulde fpeake, furely the ufe of fpeakinge would bringe oute none other fruite but plain follye and bablinge, fo that ufe is the laft and the leaft neceffarye of all three, yet nothinge can be done excellentlye withoute them all three; and therefore, *Toxophile*, I myfelfe, becaufe I never knewe whether I was apte for fhootinge or no, nor never knewe waye howe I fhould learne to fhoote, I have not ufed to fhoote : and fo, I thincke, five hundred more in *Englande* do befyde me. And furelye, if I knewe that I were apte, and you would teache me how to fhoote, I would become an archer, and the rather becaufe of the good communication, the which I have had with you this daye of fhootinge. Tox. Aptneffe, knowledge, and ufe, even as you fay, make
all

all thinges perfecte. Aptneſſe is the firſt and chiefeſt thing withoute which the other two do no good at all. Knowledge doth encreaſe all maner of aptneſſe both leſſe and more. Uſe, ſayth *Cicero*, is farre above all teaching. And thus they all three muſt be had, to do any thing very well, and if any one be away, whatſoever is done, is done very meanelye. Aptneſſe is the gift of nature, knowledge is gotten by the helpe of other; uſe lyeth in our owne diligence and labour; ſo that aptneſſe and uſe be ours and within us, through nature and labour; knowledge not ours, but comminge by other : and therefore moſt diligently of all men to be ſought for. Howe theſe three thinges ſtande with the artillerye of *Englande*, a word or two I will ſay.

All *Engliſhe* men, generally, be apt for ſhootinge and howe ? Lyke as that grounde is plentiful and fruitful, which, without any tillinge, bringeth out corne; as, for example, if a man ſhoulde goe to the mill or market with corne, and happen to ſpill ſome in the waye, yet it would take roote and growe, becauſe the ſoyle is ſo good ; ſo *Englande* may be thought very fruitful, and apte to bringe out ſhooters, where children, even from the craddle love it, and yonge men, without any teaching, ſo
diligently

diligently ufe it. Again, likewife, as a good ground, well tylled and well hufbanded, bringeth out great plenty of byg eared corne, and good to the faule: fo if the youthe of *Englande*, beinge apte of itfelfe to fhoote, were taught and learned howe to fhoote, the archers of *Englande* fhould not be onely a great deale ranker, and mo than they be; but alfo a good deale bigger and ftronger archers than they be. This commodity fhould folowe alfo, if the youthe of *Englande* were taughte to fhoote, that even as plowinge of a good grounde for wheate, doth not only make it meete for the feede, but alfo ryveth and plucketh up by the rootes all thiftles, brambles and weeds, which growe of their own accorde, to the deftruction of both corne and grounde: Even fo fhould the teachinge of youthe to fhoote, not only make them fhoote well, but alfo plucke awaye by the rootes all other defyre to noughtye paftimes, as dyfinge, cardinge, and boulinge, which without any teaching, are ufed every where, to the great harme of all youth of this realme. And likewife, as burning of thiftles, and diligente weeding them out of the corne, doth not halfe fo much rydde them, as when the ground is falloed and tilled for good grayne, as I have heard many a good hufbandman faye: even fo, neither hote punifhment,

Q   nor

nor yet diligent searching out of such unthriftinesse
by the officers, shall so thorowly weede these ungratious games out of the realme, as occupying
and bringing up youth in shootinge, and other honest pastime.   Thirdly, as a grounde which is apt
for corne, and also well tilled for corne ; yet if a
man let it lye still, and do not occupy it three or
four yeare ; but then will sowe it, if it be wheat, sayth
Columella, it will turn into rye : so if a man be
never so apt to shoote, nor never so well taughte
in his youth to shoote, yet if he geve it over, and
not use to shoote, truly when he shall be eyther
compelled in warre time for his countrys sake, or
else provoked at home for his pleasure sake, to faule
to his bowe : he shall become of a fayre archer, a
starke squyrter and dribber.   Therefore in shootinge, as in all other thinges, there can neither be
many in number, nor excellent in deede, excepte
these three thinges, aptnesse, knowledge, and use,
go together.

PHI. Very well sayd, *Toxophile*, and I promise
you, I agree to this judgement of yours together,
and therefore I cannot little marveile, why *Englishe*
men bringe no more helpe to shootinge, than nature itselfe geveth them.   For you see that even
children

children be put to their own fhiftes in fhootinge, havinge nothinge taughte them : but that they may choofe, and chaunce to fhoot ill, rather then well, unaptlye foner then fitlye, untowardlye more eafely then well favoredly, which thinge caufeth many never begin to fhoote, and mo to leave it off when they have begun : and moft of all to fhoote both worfe and weaker than they might fhoote, if they were taught.

But peradventure fome men will fay, that with ufe of fhootinge a man fhall learn to fhoote ; true it is, he fhall learne, but what fhall he learne ? Mary to fhoote noughtlie. For all ufe, in all thinges, if it be not ftayed by cunning, will very eafely bring a man to do that thing, whatfoever he goeth about, with much ilfavorednefse and defor-mitye. Which thinge how much harme it doth in learninge, both *Craffus* excellently doth prove in *Tully*, and I myfelfe have experience in my litle fhootinge. And therefore, *Toxophile*, you muft needes graunt me, that eyther *Englifhe* men do ill, in not joyning knowledge of fhootinge to ufe, or els there is no knowledge or cunning which can be gathered of fhootinge.

Q 2   Tox.

Tox. Learning to fhoote is little regarded in *Englande*, for this confideration, becaufe men be fo apte by nature they have a greate ready forwardneffe and will to ufe it, although no man teache them, although no man bidde them, and fo of their own courage they runne hedlynge on it, and fhoote they ill, fhoote they well, greet heede they take not. And, in verye deede, aptneffe with ufe may do fomewhat without knowledge, but not the tenthe parte, if fo be they were joyned with knowledge. Which three thinges be feparate as you fee, not of their owne kinde, but through the negligence of men which coupled them not together. And where ye doubt, whether there can be gathered any knowledge or arte in fhootinge or no, furelye I thincke that a man, being well exercifed in it, and fomewhat honeftlye learned withall, might foone, with diligent obferving and marking the whole nature of fhootinge, find out, as it were, an art of it, as artes in other matters have bene founde out afore, feeing that fhootinge ftandeth by thofe thinges, which may both be thorowlye perceyved, and perfectly knowen, and fuch that never fails, but be ever certaine, belonging to one moft perfect ende, as fhooting ftraight and keeping of a lengthe bringe a man to hitte the marke, the chiefe ende in fhootinge, which two thinges a man

maye

maye attaine unto, by dyligente ufinge and well
handeling thofe inftrumentes which belonge unto
them. Therefore I cannot fee, but there lyeth
hidde in the nature of fhootinge an arte, which,
by noting and obferving of them that is exercifed
in it, if he be any thing learned at all, may be
taught, to the great furtheraunce of artillerye
throughe oute all this realme: and truely I mar-
veil greatlye, that *Englifhe* men woulde never yet
feeke for the arte of fhootinge, feeinge they be fo
apt unto it, fo prayfed of their friendes, fo feared
of their enemies for it. [10] *Vegetius* would have maifters appointed, which fhould teache youthe to
fhoote fayre. [1] *Leo* the Emperour of *Rome* fheweth
the fame cuftome to have been always amongeft
the olde *Romaines:* which cuftome of teachinge
youth to fhoote, (fayth he) after it was omitted
and litle hede taken of, brought the whole empyre
of *Rome* to greate ruine. [2] *Schola Perfica,* that is,
the fchole of the *Perfians,* appointed to bringe up
youth, whiles they were twenty yeare olde, only
in fhootinge, is as notably knowne in hiftoryes as
the empyre of the *Perfians:* which fchole, as doth
appear in [3] *Cornelius Tacitus,* as fone as they gave
over and fell to other idle paftimes, broughte both

[10] Vegetius. [1] Leo. 6. 5. [2] Strabo. 11. [3] Cor. Tac. 2.

them and the *Parthians* under the fubjection of the *Romaines*. [4] *Plato* would have *common maifters and ftipendes, for to teache youthe to fhoote, and, for the fame purpofe, he would have a broade fielde neare everye citie, made common for men to ufe fhootinge in.* Whiche fayinge, the more reafonablye it is fpoken of *Plato* the more unreafonable is their deede, which would ditche up thofe fieldes privatelye for their own profite, which lyeth open generallye for the common ufe : men by fuch goods be made richer, not honefter, fayth [5] *Tullye*. If men be perfuaded to have fhootinge taughte, this authoritye which foloweth will perfwade them, or elfe none, and that is, as I have ones fayde before, of King *David*, whofe firft acte and ordinaunce was, after he was Kinge, that all *Judea* fhould learne to fhoote. If fhootinge coulde fpeake, fhe woulde accufe *Englande* of unkindneffe and flothfulneffe : of unkindneffe toward her, becaufe fhe beinge left to a little blind ufe, lackes her beft maintainer which is cunninge : of flothfulneffe towarde their owne felfe, becaufe they are content with that which aptneffe and ufe doth graunt them in fhootinge, and will feek for no knowledge as other noble common wealthes have done : and the juftlier fhooting might

[4] De leg. 7.   [5] De Offic. 2.

make

make this complaint, feeinge that of fence and weapons there is made an arte, a thinge in no wyfe to be compared to fhootinge. For of fence, almoft in everye towne, there is not onely maifters to teach it, with his provofters, ufhers, fcholers, and other names of arte and fchole, but there hath not fayled alfo, which hath diligentlye and * favouredlye written it, and is fet out in printe, that everye man maye reade it.

What difcommoditye doth come by the lacke of knowledge, in fhootinge, it were over long to rehearfe. For manye that have been apte, and loved fhootinge, becaufe they knewe not whiche waye to houlde to come to fhootinge, have cleane turned themfelves from fhootinge. And I maye tell you, *Philologe*, the lacke of teachinge to fhoote in *Englande* caufeth very many men to play with the Kinges actes, as a man did ones, eyther with the Mayor of *London* or *York*, I cannot tell whether, which did commaund by proclamation, every man in the citye to hange a lanterne, with a candell, afore his dore : which thinge the man did, but he did not light it; and fo many bye bowes, becaufe of the † acte, but yet they fhoote not, not of evil

* Favouredlye is, we fuppofe, plaufibly.   † The ftatute.

will, but becaufe they knowe not howe to fhoote. But, to conclude of this matter, in fhootinge as in all other thinges, [6] aptneffe is the firft and chiefe thinge, which if it be awaye, neyther cunninge nor ufe doth any good at all, as the *Scottes* and *Frenchmen*, with knowledge and ufe of fhootinge, fhall become good archers, when a cunninge fhip-wright fhall make a ftrong fhippe of a fallowe tree; or when a hufbandman fhall become riche, with fowinge wheat on *Newmarket* heath. [7] Cunninge muft be had, both to fet out and amend nature, and alfo to overfee and correct ufe, which ufe, if it be not led, and governed with cunning, fhall foner go amiffe, than ftraight. Ufe maketh perfitneffe in doing that thinge, whereunto nature maketh a man apt, and knowledge maketh a man cunninge before. So that it is not fo doubtful, which of them three hath moft ftroke in fhootinge, as it is plaine and evidente, that all three muft be had in excellent fhootinge. PHI. For this communication, *Toxophile*, I am very glad, and that for mine own fake, becaufe I truft now to become a fhooter. And indede I thought afore, *Englifhe* men moft apt for fhootinge, and I faw them dailye ufe fhootinge, but yet I never found none, that would talke of

[6] Aptneffe. [7] Cunninge.

anye

anye knowledge whereby a man might come to shootinge. Therefore I trust that you, by the use you have had in shootinge, have so thorowly marked and noted the nature of it, that you can teache me, as it were by a trade or way, how to come to it.

Tox. I graunt I have used shootinge metelye well: that I might have marked it well enough, if I had bene diligent. But my much shootinge hath caused me studye litle, so that thereby I lacke learninge, which should set out the art or waye in anye thinge. And you know that I was never so well seene, in the *Posteriorums* of *Aristotle*, as to invent and search out general demonstrations, for the settinge forth of any new science. Yet, by my trouth, if you will, I will go with you into the fieldes at any time, and tell you as much as I can, or els you maye stande some time at the prickes and loke on them which shoote best, and so learne. PHI. Howe litle you have loked of *Aristotle*, and howe much learninge you have lost by shootinge, I cannot tell, but this I would saye, and if I loved you never so ill, that you have been occupyed in some what els besyde shootinge. But, to our purpose, as I will not require a trade in shootinge to be taught me after the subtiltye of *Aristotle*, even so do I not agree with you in this point, that you would have me

R   learne

learne to fhoote with lokinge on them which fhoote beft, for fo I know I fhould never come to fhoote metelye; for in fhootinge, as in all other thinges which be gotten by teachinge, there muft be fhewed a way, and a path, which fhall leade a man to the beft and chiefeft point which is in fhootinge, which you do mark yourfelfe well enough, and uttered it alfo in your communication, when you fayd there lay hid in the nature of fhootinge a certaine waye which, well perceyved and thoroughlye known, would bring a man, without any wanderinge, to the beft ende in fhootinge, which you called hittinge of the pricke. Therefore I would refer all my fhootinge to that ende which is beft, and fo fhould I come the foner to fome meane. That which is beft hath no faulte, nor cannot be amended. So fhewe me befte fhootinge, not the befte fhooter, which if he be never fo good, yet hath he many a faulte, eafilye of any man to be efpyed. And therefore marveile not if I requyre to folowe that example which is without faulte, rather than that which hath fo manye faultes. And this way everye wyfe man doth folowe in teachinge any maner of thinge. As *Ariftotle*, when he teacheth a man to be good, he fettes not before him *Socrates* lyfe, which was the beft man, but chief goodnefs
itfelfe;

itfelfe ; according to which he would have a man
direct his life.   Tox. This way which you requyre
of me, *Philologe*, is to harde for me, and to hye
for a fhooter to taulke on, and taken, as I fuppofe,
out of the middeft of *Philofophie*, to fearche out
the perfite ende of any thinge, the which perfite
ende to finde out, fayth [8] *Tullye*, is the hardeft
thinge in the world, the onlye occafion and caufe
why fo many fectes of *Philofophers* hath bene alwayes
in learninge.   And although, as *Cicero* fayth, a
man maye imagine and dreame in his minde
of a perfect ende in any thinge, yet there is no experience nor ufe of it, nor was never feene yet
amonges men ; as always to heale the ficke, evermore to leade a fhippe without daunger, at all
times to hit the * pricke, fhall no phifitian, no
fhip-maifters, no fhooter ever do ; and [9] *Ariftotle*
fayth, that in all deedes there are two points to be
marked, poffibilitye and excellencye, but chieflye
a wyfe man muft folowe, and laye hande on poffibilitye, for feare he lofe both.   Therefore, feeinge that which is moft perfect and beft in fhootinge, as alwayes to hit the pricke, was never feene

[8] Orat. ad Bru.   [9] Arift. Pol. 8. 6.

* The pricke, at other times called the white, is the white fpot or point in
the midft of the mark.

R 2

nor

nor hard tell on yet amonges men, but onlye imagined and thought upon in a mans minde, me
thincke this is the wyſeſt counſell, and beſt for us
to folowe rather that which a man may come to,
than that which is unpoſſible to be attayned to, leſt
juſtlye that ſayinge of the wyſe *Iſmene* in *Sophocles*
maye be verifyed on us.

A foole is he that takes in hande he cannot ende.   Soph. Ant.

PHI. Well, if the perfite ende of other matters
had bene as perfitelye knowne, as the perfite ende
of ſhootinge is, there had never bene ſo many ſects
of *Philoſophers* as there be, for in ſhootinge both
man and boy is of one opinion, that alwayes to hit
the pricke is the moſt perfite ende that can be imagined, ſo that we ſhall not neede greatly contende in
this matter. But nowe, Sir, whereas you thincke
that a man in learninge to ſhoote, or any thinge
els, ſhould rather wyſelye folowe poſſibilitye, than
vainly ſeke for perfite excellencye, ſurelye I will
prove that everye wyſe man, that wyſely would
learne any thinge, ſhall chieflye go about that
whereunto he knoweth well he ſhall never come.
And you yourſelfe, I ſuppoſe, ſhall confeſſe the
ſame to be the beſt way in teaching, if you will
aunſwer me to thoſe thinges which I will aſke of
you.

you.　Tox. And that I will gladlye, both becaufe I thincke it is impoffible for you to prove it,
and alfo becaufe I defire to heare what you can
fay in it.

Phi. The ftudye of a good phifitian, *Toxophile*,
I trowe be to knowe all difeafes and all medycines
fit for them.　* Tox. It is fo indeed.　Phi.
Becaufe, I fuppofe, he would gladly, at all times,
heale all difeafes of all men.　Tox. Yea, trulye.
Phi. A good purpofe furelye, but was there ever
phifition yet amonge fo manye which hath laboured
in this ftudye, that at all times could heale all difeafes?　Tox. No truly, nor, I thincke, never
fhall be.　Phi. Then phifitions belike, ftudy
for that, which none of them commeth unto.　But
in learning of fence, I pray you what is that which
men moft labour for?　Tox. That they may
hit another, I trowe, and never take blow their
felfe.　Phi. You fay trothe, and I am fure every
one of them would fayne do fo whenfoever he
playeth.　But was there ever any of them fo cunninge yet, which, at one time or other, hath not
been touched?　Tox. The beft of them all is glad

---

* Here is an example of the Socratic method of difputaion, which, by re-
peated interrogations, confutes the opponent out of his own anfwers.

sometimes

fometimes to efcape with a blowe. PHI. Then
in fence alfo, men are taught to go about that
thinge, which the beft of them all knoweth he fhall
never attaine unto. Moreover you that be fhooters, I praye you, what meane you, when ye take
fo great heede to kepe your ftandinge, to fhoote
compaffe, to loke on your marke fo diligentlye, to
caft uppe graffe divers times, and other thinges
more you know better than I. What would you
do then, I praye you? Tox. Hit the marke if
we could. PHI. And doth every man go about
to hit the marke at every fhote? Tox. By my
trothe I trowe fo, and, as for myfelfe, I am fure I
do. PHI. But all men do not hit at all times?
Tox. No, trulye, for that were a wonder. PHI.
Can any man hit it at all times? Tox. No
man trulye. PHI. Then bylikely to hit the
pricke alwayes is unpoffible. For that is called unpoffible which is in no mans power to do. Tox.
Unpoffible indede. PHI. But to fhoote wide
and farre of the marke is a thinge poffible. Tox.
No man will denye that. PHI. But yet to hit
the marke alwayes were an excellent thinge. Tox.
Excellent furelye. PHI. Then I am fure thofe
be wyfer men which covet to fhoot wyde, than
thofe which covet to hit the pricke. Tox.
Why

Why so, I praye you? PHI. Becaufe to fhoote
wyde is a thinge poffible, and therefore, as you faye
yourfelfe, of every wyfe man to be followed. And
as for hittinge the pricke, becaufe it is unpoffible,
it were a vain thinge to go about it in good * fad-
neffe, *Toxophile*; thus you fee that a man mighte
go through all craftes and fciences, and prove that
any man in his fcience coveteth that which he fhall
never get. TOX. By my trothe (as you fay) I
cannot denye but they do fo: but why and wherefore they fhould do fo, I cannot learne. PHI.
I will tell you. Everye crafte and fcience ftandeth
in two thinges: in knowinge of his crafte, and
workinge of his crafte: for perfect knowledge bringeth a man to perfect workinge: This know paint-
ers, carvers, taylors, fhomakers, and all other
craftefmen, to be true. Now, in every crafte there
is a perfect excellencye, which may be better known
in a mans minde, than followed in a mans dede.
This perfectneffe, becaufe it is generally layed as a
brode wyde example afore all men, no one particular man is able to compaffe it: and, as it is general to all men, fo it is perpetual for all time, which
proveth it a thinge for man unpoffible: although
not for the capacitye of our thinckinge, which is

* Sadneffe is ferioufnefs, or earneft.

heavenlye,

heavenlye, yet furelye for the habilitye of our workinge, which is worldly. God geveth not full perfectneſſe to one man (ſayth 10 *Tullye*) left if one
man had all in any one ſcience, there ſhould be nothinge left for another. Yet God ſuffereth us to
have the perfect knowledge of it, that ſuch a knowledge, diligently folowed, might bringe for the accordinge as a man doth laboure, perfect workinge.
And who is he, that, in learninge to wryte, would
forſake an excellent example, and followe a worſe?
Therefore, ſeinge perfectneſſe itſelfe is an example
for us, let every man ſtudye how he may come nye
it, which is a point of wyſedome, not reaſon with
God why he may not attaine unto it, which is
vaine curioſity.

Tox. Surelye this is gaily ſaide, *Philologe*, but
yet this one thinge I am afraid of, leaſt this perfectneſſe which you ſpeake on will diſcourage men
to take any thinge in hand, becauſe, afore they begin, they know they ſhall never come to an end.
And thus diſpayre ſhall diſpatch, even at the firſt
entring it, many a good man his purpoſe and in-
tent. And I think both you yourſelfe, and all
other men to, would counte it mere follye for a

10 De Inven. 2.

man

man to tell him whom he teacheth, that he fhall never obtain that which he would fayneft learne. And therefore this fame highe and perfeᴄt way of teachinge let us leave it to higher matters, and, as for fhootinge, it fhall be contente with a meaner way well enough.　PHI. Whereas you faye that this hye perfeᴄtneffe will difcourage men, becaufe they knowe they fhall never attaine unto it, I am fure, cleane contrarye, there is nothing in the worlde fhall encourage men more than it. And why? For where a man feeth, that though another man be never fo excellent, yet it is poffible for himfelfe to be better, what payne or labour will that man refufe to take? If the game be once wonne, no man will fet forth his foote to runne. And thus perfeᴄtneffe beinge fo highe a thinge that men may looke at it, not come to it, and beinge fo plentifull and indifferent to every body, that the plentifulneffe of it may provoke all men to labour, becaufe it hath enough for all men, the indifferencye of it fhall encourage every one to take more payne than his fellow, becaufe every man is rewarded accordinge to his nye comminge, and yet, which is moft marveile of all, the more men take of it, the more they leave be-

S　　　　　　　　hinde

hinde for other, as *Socrates* did in wyſedom, and *Cicero* in eloquence, whereby other hath not lacked, but hath fared a great deale the better. And thus perfectneſſe itſelfe, becauſe it is never obtained, even therefore onlye dothe it cauſe ſo manye men to be well ſeene and perfect in many matters, as they be. But whereas you thincke that it were fondneſſe to teache a man to ſhoote, in lookinge at the moſt perfectneſſe in it, but rather would have a man go ſome other waye to worke, I truſt no wyſe man will diſcommend that waye, excepte he thincke himſelfe wyſer than *Tullye*, which doth plainlye ſaye, That, if he teached anye maner of crafte, as he did Rhetoricke, he would labour to bringe a man to the [1] knowledge of the moſt perfectneſſe of it, which knowledge ſhould evermore leade and guide a man to do that thinge well which he went about. Which waye in all maner of learninge to be beſt, *Plato* doth alſo declare in *Euthydemus*, of whom *Tullye* learned it, as he did many other thinges mo. And thus you ſee, *Toxophile*, by what reaſons, and by whoſe authority I do require of you this way in teachinge me to ſhoote; which waye, I praye you, without any delaye, ſhewe me as farre forth as you have noted and marked.

[1] De Orat. 3.

Tox.

Tox. You call me to a thinge, *Philologe*, which I
am loth to do, and yet, if I do it not, beinge but
a small matter as you thincke, you will lacke friend-
shipe in me; if I take it in hande, and not bringe
it to passe as you would have it, you might thincke
greate want of wysedome in me.

But I advyse you, seeing you will needes have it
so, the blame shall be yours, as well as myne :
yours for puttinge uppon me so * instauntly : myne
for receyvinge so fondlye a greater burthen than I
am able to bear. Therefore I, more willinge to
fulfil your minde than hopinge to accomplishe that
which you loke for, shall speake of it, not as a
maister of shootinge, but as one not altogether ignorant in shootinge. And one thing I am glad of,
the sunne drawinge down so fast into the West
shall compell me to drawe apace to the ende of our
matter, so that his darknesse shall something cloke
myne ignoraunce.

And because you knowe the orderinge of a
matter better than I, aske me generallye of it,
and I shall particularly answere to it. PHI.

* So importunately.

S 2   Very

Very gladly, *Toxophile* : for ſo by order thoſe thinges which I would know, you ſhall tell the better; and thoſe thinges which you ſhall tell, I ſhall remember the better.

THE END OF THE FIRST BOOKE OF THE

SCHOLE OF SHOOTINGE.

TOXOPHILUS.

TOXOPHILUS.

THE

SECONDE BOOKE

OF THE

SCHOLE OF SHOOTINGE.

PHILOLOGUS.   TOXOPHILUS.

PHI. WHAT is the chiefe pointe in fhootinge, that every man laboureth to
come to? Tox. To hit the marke. PHI.
How manye thinges are required to make a
man evermore hit the marke? Tox. Two.
PHI. Which two? Tox. Shootinge ftreighte,
and kepinge of a lengthe. PHI. How fhould a
man fhoote ftreight, and how fhould a man keep
a lengthe? Tox. In knowinge and havinge
thinges belonginge to fhootinge; and when they be
knowen and had in well handlinge of them; whereof
fome belonge to fhootinge ftreight, fome to kepinge of a lengthe, fome commonlye to them
both,

both, as ſhall be tolde ſeverallye of them in place convenient.

PHI. Thinges belonginge to ſhootinge, which be they?

TOX. * All thinges be outwarde; and ſome be inſtrumentes for every † ſere archer to bringe with him, proper for his owne uſe: other thinges be general to every man, as the place and time ſerveth. PHI. Which be inſtrumentes? TOX. Bracer, ſhoottinge glove, ſtringe, bowe, and ſhafte. PHI. Which be general to all men? TOX. The weather and the marke, yet the marke is ever under the rule of the weather. PHI. Wherein ſtandeth well handlinge of thinges? TOX. Alltogether within a man himſelfe, ſome handlinge is proper to inſtrumentes, ſome to the wether, ſome to the marke, ſome is within a man himſelfe. PHI. What handlinge is proper to the inſtrumentes? TOX. Standinge, nockinge, drawinge, holdinge, lowſinge, whereby commeth fayre ſhootinge, which neyther belonge to winde nor wether, nor yet to the marke, for in a raine and at no marke, a man may ſhoote a fayre ſhote.

* The inſtruments of ſhooting are external. † Sere is ſeveral or particular.

PHI.

PHI. Well sayd, what handlinge belongeth to the wether? Tox. Knowinge of his winde, with him, against him, syde winde, full syde winde, syde winde quarter with him, syde winde quarter against him, and so forthe. PHI. Well then go to, what handlinge belongeth to the mark? Tox. To marke his standinge, to shoote compasse, to drawe evermore like, to louse evermore like, to consider the nature of the pricke, in hilles and dales, in strayte plaines and windinge places, and also to espye his marke. PHI. Very well done. And what is only within a man himselfe? Tox. Good heede gevinge, and avoydinge all affections: which thinges oftentimes do marre and make all. And these thinges spoken of me generally and brieflye, if they be well knowen, had, and handled, shall bringe a man to suche shootinges, as fewe or none ever yet came unto, but surely if he misse in anye one of them, he can never hitte the marke, and in the more he doth misse, the farther he shooteth from his marke. But, as in all other matters, the first steppe or stayre to be good, is to knowe a mans faulte, and then to amende it, and he that will not knowe his faulte, shall never amende it. PHI. You speake nowe, *Toxophile*, even as I woulde have you to speake; but let us returne againe unto our

matter,

matter, and thofe thinges which you have packed up in fo fhort a roume, we will loufe them forth, and take every piece, as it were, in our hande, and loke more narrowlye upon it.

Tox. I am content, but we will rýdde them as faft as we can, becaufe the funne goeth fo faft downe, and yet fomewhat muft needes be fayd of every one of them.   Phi. Well faid, and I trowe we beganne with thofe thinges which be inftrumentes, whereof the firft, as I fuppofe, was the bracer.

Tox. Little is to be fayd of the [2] bracer. A * bracer ferveth for two caufes, one to fave his arme from the ftrype of the ftringe, and his doublet from wearing ; and the other is, that the ftringe glidinge fharplye and quicklye of the bracer, maye make the fharper fhoote.   For if the ftringe fhoulde lighte upon the bare fleve, the ftrengthe of the fhoote fhould ftoppe and dye there.   But it is befte, by my judgmente, to geve the bowe fo muche bent,

[2] Bracer.

* Thofe who write of things well known, feldom extend their care to time in which they may be known lefs. This account of the bracer is fomewhat obfcure. It feems to have been a kind of clofe fleeve laced upon the left arm.

that

that the ſtringe neede never touche a mans arme,
and ſo ſhoulde a man neede no bracer, as I knowe
many good archers which occupye none. In a bracer
a man muſt take hede of three thinges, that it have
no nayles in it, that it have no buckles, that it be faſt
on with laces without agglettes. For the nayles
will ſheere in ſunder a mans ſtringe before he be
ware, and ſo put his bowe in jeopardye: buckles
and agglettes at unawares, ſhall race his bowe, a
thinge both evill for the ſighte, and perillous for
freatinge. And thus a bracer is only had for this
purpoſe, that the ſtringe maye have redye paſſage.

Phi. In my bracer I am cunninge enoughe, but
what ſay you of the ³ ſhootinge glove? Tox.
A ſhootinge glove is chieflye for to ſave a mans
fingers from hurtinge, that he maye be able to
beare the ſharpe ſtringe to the uttermoſte of his
ſtrengthe. And when a man ſhooteth, the might
of his ſhoote lyeth on the foremoſt finger, and on
the ringman, for the middle finger, which is the
longeſt, like a lubber, ſtarteth backe, and beareth
no weight of the ſtringe in a manner at all, therefore the two other fingers muſt have thicker leather,
and that muſt have thickeſt of all, whereon a man

³ Shootinge glove.

T   lowſeth

lowſeth moſt, and for ſure lowſinge, the formoſt
finger is moſt apt, becauſe it holdeſt beſt, and for
that purpoſe, nature hath, as a man would ſay,
yocked it with the thoumbe.   Leather, if it be next
a mans ſkinne, will ſweate, waxe harde and chafe,
therefore ſcarlet, for the ſoftneſſe of it and thick-
neſſe withall, is good to ſewe within a mannes glove.
If that will not ſerve, but your finger hurteth, you
muſt take a ſearing cloth, made of fine virgin waxe,
and deres ſewet, and put next your finger, and ſo
on with your glove.   If yet you feele your finger
pinched, leave ſhootinge, both becauſe then you
ſhall ſhoote nought, and againe by little and little,
hurtinge your finger, ye ſhall make it longe and
longe to or you ſhoote againe.   A newe glove
pluckes manye ſhootes, becauſe the ſtringe goeth
not frelye of, and therefore the fingers muſt be
cutte ſhorte, and trimmed with ſome ointment,
that the ſtringe maye glyde well away.   Some with
holding in the nocke of their ſhafte harde, rubbe
the ſkinne of their fingers.   For this there be two
remedyes, one to have a gooſe quill * ſpinetted
and ſewed againſt the nockinge, betwixt the lyninge
and the leather, which ſhall helpe the ſhoote much
to ; the other way is to have ſome roule of leather

* Spinetted is perhaps ſlit and opened.

ſewed

sewed betwixt his fingers, at the setting on of the fingers, which shall kepe his fingers so in sunder, that they shall not holde the nocke so fast as they did. The shootinge glove hath a purse, which shall serve to put fine linen clothe and waxe in, two necessarye thinges for a shooter. Some men use gloves, or other such like thinge on theyr bow-hand for chafinge, because they hold so hard. But that cometh commonly when a bow is not round, but somewhat square; fine waxe shall do verye well in such a case to lay where a man holdeth his bow: and thus much as concerninge your glove.

And these thinges, although they be trifles, yet because you be but a yonge shooter, I would not leave them out.   PHI. And so you shall do me most pleasure. The [4] stringe, I trowe, be the next.   TOX. The next indeede; a thinge thoughe it be litle, yet not a litle to be regarded.   But herein you must be content to put your trust in honest string-ers.   And surelye stringers ought more diligentlye to be loked upon by the officers, than eyther bower or fletcher, because they may deceyve a simple man the more easelyer.   An ill stringe breaketh many a good bowe, nor no other thinge halfe so manye.

[4] Stringe.

T 2

In

In warre, if a ftringe breake the man is loft, and is no man, for his weapon is gone, and although he have two ftringes put on at once, yet he fhall have fmall leafure and leffe roume to bende his bowe, therefore God fend us good ftringers both for warre and peace. Now what a ftringe ought to be made on, whether of good hempe, as they do nowe a dayes, or of flaxe, or of filke, I leave that to the judgement of ftringers, of whom we muft buy them. [5] *Euftathius*, upon this verfe of *Homer*,

---

* Twang the bowe, and twang the ftring, out quicklie the fhaft flue. Iliad 4.

---

doth tell, that, in oulde time, they made theyr bowe ftringes of bullox † thermes, which they twined together as they do ropes, and therefore they made a greate twange. Bow ftringes alfo hath bene made of the heare of an horfe tayle, called, for the matter of them, *Hippias*, as doth appeare in manye good authors of the [6] *Greeke* tongue. Great ftringes and litle ftringes be for divers purpofes : the great ftring is more furer for the bowe, more ftable to pricke withall, but flower for the caft. The litle ftring is cleane contrarye, not fo

[5] Euftathius. [6] Favorinus.

* Perhaps this line fhould ftand thus,
' Twang the bow, and twang went the ftring, out quickly the fhaft flue.'

† Thermes or tharms are guts.

sure,

sure, therefore to be taken heede of, left with longe
taryinge on, it breake your bowe, more fit to fhoote
farre, than apt to pricke neare, therefore when you
know the nature of both bigge and litle, you muft
fit your bowe accordinge to the occafion of your
fhootinge. In stringinge of your bowe (though
this place belonge rather to the handlinge than to
the thinge itfelfe, yet becaufe the thinge, and the
handlinge of the thinge, be fo joyned together, I
muft needes fometimes couple the one with the
other) you muft marke the fit length of your bowe.
For, if the ftringe be too fhorte, the bendinge will
geve, and at the laft flyp, and fo put the bowe in
jeopardye. If it be longe, the bendinge muft nedes
be in the fmall of the ftringe, which beinge fore
twyned, muft needes knap in funder, to the deftruction of manye good bowes. Moreover, you
muft looke that your bowe be well nocked, for
feare the fharpneffe of the horne fhere afunder the
ftringe. And that chaunceth oft when in bending,
the ftringe hath but one way to ftrength it withall.
You muft marke alfo to fet your ftringe ftreighte
on, or els the one ende fhall wrieth contrarye to
the other, and fo breake your bowe. When the
ftringe beginneth never fo litle to weare, truft it
not, but away with it, for it is an yll faved half-
penny,

peny, that coftes a man a crowne. Thus you fee
how many jeopardyes hangeth over the felye poore
bow, by reafon onlye of the ftringe. As when the
ftringe is fhorte, when it is longe, when eyther of
the nockes be noughte, when it hath but one way,
and when it taryeth over longe on.

PHI. I fee weil it is no marveile, though fo many
bowes be broken. Tox. Bowes be broken twyfe
as many wayes befyde thefe. But againe in ftring-
inge your bowe, you muft loke for much bende or
litle bende, for they be cleane contrarye. The litle
bende hath but one commoditye, which is in fhootinge fafter, and farther fhoote, and the caufe thereof
is, becaufe the ftringe hath fo farre a paffage, or it
part with the fhaft. The great bende hath many
commodities: for it maketh eafyer fhooting, the
bow beinge half drawen afore. It needeth no
bracer, for the ftringe ftoppeth before it come at
the arme. I will not fo fone hit a mans fleve or
other geare, by the fame reafon. It hurteth not
the fhaft fether, as the low bend doth. It fuffereth
a man better to efpie his marke. Therefore let
your bowe have good bigge bende, a fhaftment and
two fingers at the leaft, for thefe which I have
fpoken of.

PHI.

PHI. The bracer, glove, and ſtringe, be done, nowe you muſt come to the ⁷ bowe, the chiefe inſtrument of all.   TOX. Dyvers countryes and tymes have uſed alwayes dyvers bowes, and of dyvers faſhions.   Horne bowes are uſed in ſome places now, and were uſed alſo in *Homerus* dayes, for *Pandarus* bowe, the beſt ſhooter amonge all the *Troyans*, was made of two goate hornes joyned together, the lengthe whereof, ſayth ⁸ *Homer*, was ſixteen handbredes, not farre differinge from the lengthe of our bowes. ⁹ Scripture maketh mention of braſſe bowes. Iron bowes, and ſtele bowes, have bene of longe time, and alſo now are uſed among the *Turkes*, but yet they muſt nedes be unprofitable.   For if braſſe, iron, or ſtele, have their owne ſtrengthe and pithe in them, they be farre above mans ſtrengthe : if they be made meete for mans ſtrengthe, theyr pithe is nothinge worth to ſhoote any ſhoote withall. The ¹⁰ *Ethiopians* had bowes of palme tree, which ſeemed to be very ſtronge, but we have none experience of them.   The length of them was four cubites.   The men of *Inde* had theyr bowes made of a rede, which was of a great ſtrength.   And no marveile thoughe bowe and ſhaftes were made

7 Bowe. ⁸ Iliad. 4. ⁹ Pſalme 17. ¹⁰ Hera. in Pol.

thereof,

thereof, for the redes be so greate in *Inde*, as
[1] *Herodotus* sayth, that of everye joynte of a rede
a man may make a fishers bote. These bowes,
sayth [2] *Arrianus* in *Alexanders* life, gave so greate
a stroke, that no harnesse or buckler, thoughe it
were never so stronge, could withstande it. The
length of such a bowe was even with the length of
him that used it. The *Lycians* used bowes made
of a tree, called in *Latine* [3] *Cornus*, (as concerninge
the name of it in *Englishe*, I can soner prove that
other men call it false, than I can tell the right name of
it myselfe) this wodde is as harde as horne, and verye
fitte for shaftes, as shall be toulde after. *Ovid* sheweth that [4] *Syrinx* the *Nymphe*, and one of the mayd-
ens of *Diana*, had a bowe of this wodde, whereby the
poet meaneth, that it was very excellent to make
bowes of.

As for Brasell, Elme, Wych, and Ashe, experience doth prove them to be but meane for bowes,
and so to conclude, Ewe of all other thinges is
that, whereof perfite shootinge would have a bowe
made. This wodde, as it is nowe generall and common amonges *Englishmen*, so hath it continued
from long time, and had in most price for bowes,

[1] In Thal. [2] Arrianus 8. [3] In Polym. [4] Metam. 1.

amonges

amonges the *Romaines,* as doth appeare in this halfe verſe of *Virgill.*

Taxi torquentur in arcus. *Virgilius.*

Ewe fit for a bowe to be made on.

Nowe, as I ſaye, a bowe of Ewe muſt be made for perfecte ſhootinge at the prickes, which marke, becauſe it is certaine, and moſt certaine rules may be geven of it, ſhall ſerve for our communication at this time. A good bowe is knowen, much what as good counſayle is knowen, by the ende and profite of it ; yet both a bowe and good counſayle may be made both better and worſe, by well or ill handlinge of them, as oftentimes chaunceth. And as a man both muſt and will take counſayle of a wyſe and honeſt man, though he ſee not the ende of it; ſo muſt a ſhooter, of neceſſitye, truſt an honeſt and good bowyer for a bowe, afore he knowe the proofe of it. And as a wyſe man will take plenty of counſayle aforehande, whatſoever neede, ſo a ſhooter ſhould have alwayes three or four bowes in ſtore, whatſoever chaunce. PHI. But if I truſt bowyers alwayes, ſometimes I am like to be deceyved. TOX. Therefore ſhall I tell you ſome tokens in a bowe, that you ſhall be the ſeldomer deceyved. If you come into a ſhoppe, and find a

U   bowe

bowe that is fmall, longe, heavye, and ftronge, lyinge ftreighte, not windinge, not marred with knotte
gaule, winde fhake, wem, freat or pinch, bye that
bowe of my warrante. The befte colour of a bowe
that I finde, is when the backe and the bellye in
workinge be much what after one maner, for fuch
oftentimes in wearinge do prove like virgin waxe
or golde, havinge a fine longe graine, even from the
one ende of the bowe to the other; the fhorte graine,
although fuch prove well fometimes, are for the
moft part very brittle. Of the makinge of the
bowe, I will not greatly meddle, left I fhould feeme
to enter into an other mans occupation, which I
cannot fkill of. Yet I would defyre all bowyers to
feafon theyr ftaves well, to work them and fynke
them well, to geve them heetes conveniente, and
tylleringes plentye. For thereby they fhould both
gette themfelves a good name, (and a good
name encreafeth a mans profite muche) and alfo do
great commoditye to the hole realme. If anye
man do offende in this poynte, I am afraid they be
thofe journeymen, which laboure more fpedelye to
make many bowes for their moneye fake, than they
work diligentlye to make good bowes, for the common wealth fake, not layinge before theyr eyes this
wyfe proverbe, *Sone enoughe, if well enoughe*; where-

with

with every honeſt handy craftes man ſhould mea-
ſure, as it were with a rule, his worke withall.   He
that is a journeyman, and rydeth upon another
mans horſe, if he ryde an honeſt pace, no man will
diſalowe him : but if he make poſte haſte, both he
that owneth the horſe, and he peradventure alſo
that afterward ſhall bye the horſe, may chaunce to
curſe him.   Such haſtineſſe, I am afrayde, may alſo
be founde amonge ſome of them, which throughe
oute the realme, in divers places, worke the Kinges
artillerye for warre, thinking, if they get a bow or
a ſheafe of arrowes to ſome faſhion, they be good
enough for bearing gere.   And thus that weapon,
which is the chiefe defence of the realme, verye oft
doth little ſervice to him that ſhould uſe it, becauſe
it is ſo negligently wrought of him that ſhould make
it, when trulye I ſuppoſe that neither the bowe can
be too good and chiefe woode, nor yet too well
ſeaſoned or truly made, with hetinges and tiller-
inges, neither that ſhafte too good wodde, or too
thorowly wroughte, with the beſt pinion fethers
that can be gotten, wherewith a man ſhall ſerve his
Prince, defende his countrye, and ſave himſelfe
from his enemye.   And I truſt no man will be
angrye with me for ſpeakinge thus, but thoſe which
finde, themſelves touched therein : which ought ra-

ther

ther to be angrye with themſelves for doinge, than
to be miſcontent with me for ſayinge ſo. And in
no caſe they ought to be diſpleaſed with me, ſeeinge
this is ſpoken alſo after that ſort, not for the no-
tinge of any perſon ſeverallye, but for the amend-
inge of everye one generallye.

But turne we againe to know a good ſhootinge bowe for our purpoſe. Everye bow is made
eyther of a boughe, of a plante, or of the boole of
the tree. The boughe commonlye is very knottye,
and full of pinnes, weake, of ſmall pithe, and ſone
will folowe the ſtringe, and ſeldome werith to anye
fayre coloure, yet for children and yong beginners
it may ſerve well enough. The plant proveth many
times well, if it be of a good and cleane groweth,
and, for the pithe of it, is quicke enoughe of caſt,
it will plye and bowe farre before it breake, as all
other yonge thinges do. The boole of the tree is
cleaneſt without knot or pin, having a faſt and harde
wodde, by reaſon of his full groweth, ſtrong and
mightye of caſte, and beſt for a bowe, if the ſtaves
be even cloven, and be afterwarde wrought, not
overthwart the woode, but as the graine and ſtreight
growinge of the woode leadeth a man, or els, by
all reaſon, it muſt ſone breake, and that in many
ſhivers.

ſhivers. This muſt be conſidered in the roughe woode, and when the bowe ſtaves be over wroughte and faſhioned. For in dreſſinge and pykinge it up for a bowe, it is too late to loke for it.

But yet in theſe pointes, as I ſayde before, you muſt truſt an honeſte bowyer, to put a good bowe in your hand, ſomewhat lokinge yourſelfe to thoſe tokens I ſhewed you. And you muſt not ſticke for a grote or twelve pence more than another man would geve, if it be a good bowe. For a good bowe twiſe paid for, is better than an ill bowe once broken.

Thus a ſhooter muſt begin, not at the makinge of his bowe, like a bowyer, but at the byinge of his bowe, like an archer. And, when his bowe is boughte and broughte home, afore he truſt much upon it, let him trye and trimme it after this ſort.

Take your bowe into the fielde, ſhoote in him, fincke him with deade heavye ſhaftes, looke where he cometh moſte, provide for that place betimes, leaſt it pinche, and ſo freate : when you have thus ſhotte in him, and perceyved good ſhootinge woode in him, you muſt have him againe to a good, cun-ninge,

ninge, and trufty workman, which fhall cutte him
fhorter, and pike him and dreffe him fitter, make him
come round compaffe every where, and whipping
at the endes, but with difcretion, leaft he whippe
in funder, or els freete, foner than he is ware of:
he muft alfo laye him ftreight, if he be cafte, or
otherwife neede requyre, and if he be flatte made,
gather him rounde, and fo fhall he both fhoote the
fafter, for farre fhootinge, and alfo be furer for
near prickinge.   PHI. What if I come into a
fhoppe, and fpye out a bowe, which fhall both
then pleafe me very well when I bye him, and be
alfo very fitte and meete for me when I fhoote in
him: fo that he be both weak enoughe for eafy
fhootinge, alfo quicke and fpeedye enoughe for farre
caftinge, then, I would thincke, I fhall neede no
more bufinefs with him, but be content with him,
and ufe him well enoughe, and fo, by that means,
avoyde both great trouble, and alfo fome coft, which
you cunninge archers very often put yourfelves
unto, beinge verye *Englifhmen*, never ceafinge pid-
deling about theyr bowe and fhaftes, when they be
well, but eyther with fhortinge and pykinge your
bowes, or els with newe featheringe, peecinge and
headinge your fhaftes, can never have done untill
they be ftarke noughte.   Tox. Well, *Philologe*,
furelye

surelye if I have any judgmente at all in fhootinge, it is no very great good taken in a bow, whereof nothinge when it is new and frefh neede be cutte away, even as *Cicero* fayth of a younge mans witte and ftyle, which you know better than I. For every newe thinge muft alwayes have more than it needeth, or els it will not waxe better and better, but ever decaye, and be worfe and worfe. Newe ale, if it runne not over the barrel when it is newe tunned, will fone leafe his * pithe, and his heade afore he be longe drawen on. And likewyfe as that colte, which, at the firft takinge up, needeth litle breakinge and handlinge, but is fitte and gentle enoughe for the faddle, feldome or never proveth well: even fo that bowe, which at the firft byinge, without any more proof and trimminge, is fitte and eafye to fhoote in, fhall neyther be profitable to lafte longe, nor yet pleafant to fhoote well. And therefore as a young horfe full of courage, with handlinge and breakinge, is brought unto a fure pace and goinge, fo fhall a newe bowe, frefh and quick of cafte, by finking and cutting, be broughte to a ftedfaft fhootinge. And an eafy and gentle bowe, when it is newe, is not much unlike a foft fpirited boye, when he is younge. But yet, as of

---

* Pithe is ftrength, fpritelinefs, vigour, power of action.

an

an unrulye boye with righte handlinge, proveth
oftenest of all a well ordered man : so of an unfit
and staffishe bowe, with good trimminge, must
nedes folowe alwayes a stedfast shootinge bowe.
And suche a perfite bowe, which never will deceive
a man, excepte a man deceyve it, must be had for
that perfecte ende, which you look for in shootinge.

PHI. Well, *Toxophile*, I see well you be cunninger in this gere than I : but put the case that I
have three or foure such good bowes, pyked and
dressed as you now speake of, yet I do remember that
many learned men do say, that it is easyer to get a
good thinge, than to save and kepe a good thinge,
wherefore, if thou can teach me as concerninge that
point, you have satisfyed me plentifullye, as concerninge a bowe.

TOX. Trulye it was the next thinge that I would
have come unto, for so the matter laye. When
you have brought your bowe to such a pointe, as I
spake of, then you must have a harden or wullen
cloth waxed, wherewith every daye you must rubbe
and chafe your bowe, till it shyne and glitter withall.
Which thinge shall cause it both to be cleane, well
favoured, goodlye of coloure, and shall also bringe,

as

as it were, a cruſte over it, that is to ſaye, ſhall make it everye where on the out ſyde, ſo ſlipperye and harde, that neyther anye weete or weather can enter to hurte it, nor yet anye freate, or pinche, be able to byte upon it : but that you ſhall do it greate wronge before you breake it. This muſt be done often-times, but eſpecially when you come from ſhootinge.

Beware alſo when you ſhoote of your ſhafte heades, dagger, knyves, or agglettes, leſt they race your bowe, a thinge, as I ſayde before, both un-ſemelye to loke on, and alſo daungerous for freates. Take heede alſo of miſtye and dankinſhe dayes, which ſhall hurt a bowe more than anye rayne. For then you muſt eyther alwaye rubbe it, or els leave ſhootinge.

Your ⁵ bowe caſe (this I did not promiſe to ſpeake of, becauſe it is without the nature of ſhoot-inge, or els I ſhould trouble me with other thinges infinite more : yet ſeinge it is a ſavegarde for the bowe, ſome thinge I will ſaye of it) your bowe caſe, I ſaye, if you ryde forthe, muſt neyther be to wyde for your bowes, for ſo ſhall one clappe uppon an other, and hurt them, nor yet ſo ſtrayte that ſcarce

⁵ Bowe caſe.

X   they

they can be thruſt in, for that would lay them on
ſyde, and wynde them. A bow caſe of lether is
not the beſt, for that is oft times moyſt, which
hurteth the bowes very much.

Therefore I have ſeene good ſhooters which
would have for everye bowe a ſere caſe, made of
wullen clothe, and then you maye putte three or
four of them ſo caſed, into a lether caſe if you will.
This wullen caſe ſhall both kepe them in ſunder,
and alſo will kepe a bowe in his full ſtrength, that
it never geve for anye weather.

At home theſe * woode caſes be verye good for
bowes to ſtande in. But take hede that your bowe
ſtande not to nere a ſtone wall, for that will make
him moyſt and weake, nor yet to neare anye fyre,
for that will make him ſhorte and brittle. And
thus much as concerninge the ſavinge and keepinge
of our bowe: now you ſhall heare what thinges ye
muſt avoyde, for fear of breakinge your bowe.

A ſhooter chaunceth to breake his bowe commonlye four wayes, by the ſtringe, by the ſhaft,

* There is no mention of wooden caſes before, therefore it ſhould perhaps
be wool caſes, unleſs ſomething be left out by the printer.

by drawinge to farre, and by freates. By the ſtringe, as I ſayd afore, when the ſtringe is eyther to ſhort, to long, not ſurelye put on, with one wappe, or juſt croked on, or ſhorne in ſunder with an evill nocke, or ſuffered to tarye over long on. When the ſtringe fayles the bowe muſt needes breake, and ſpeciallye in the middes: becauſe both the endes have nothinge to ſtoppe them: but whippes ſo farre backe, that the bellye muſt needes violently riſe up, the which you ſhall well perceyve in bendinge of a bowe backewarde. Therefore a bowe that foloweth the ſtringe is leaſt hurte with breakinge of ſtringes.

By the ſhaft a bow is broken eyther when it is to ſhort, and ſo you ſet it in your bowe, or when the nocke breakes for litleneſſe, or when the ſtringe ſlippes without the nocke for wydeneſſe, then you pull it to your eare and lettes it go, which muſt needes breake the ſhaft at the leaſt, and put ſtringe and bow and all in jeopardye, becauſe the ſtrength of the bowe hath nothinge in it to ſtoppe the violence of it. This kinde of breakinge is moſt perillous for the ſtanders by, for in ſuch a caſe you ſhall ſee ſome time the ende of a bow flye a hoole ſcore from a man, and that moſt commonly, as I have marked oft, the upper ende of the bowe.

The

The bow is drawne to farre two wayes. Eyther when you take a longer ſhaft then your owne, or els when you ſhift your hande to lowe or to hye for ſhootinge faire. This waye pulleth the backe in ſunder, and then the bowe fleeth in many peces.

So when you ſee a bowe broken, havinge the bellye riſen uppe both wayes or to one, the ſtringe brake it. When it is broken in two peces, in a maner even of, and ſpeciallye in the upper ende, the ſhaft nocke brake it. When the backe is pulled aſunder in many peces, to farre drawinge brake it. Theſe tokens eyther alwayes be true, or els very ſeldome miſſe.

The fourthe thinge that breaketh a bowe is [6] freates, which make a bowe redye and apt to breake by any of the three wayes afore ſayde. Freates be in a ſhaft as well as in a bowe, and they be much like a canker, creepinge and encreaſinge in thoſe places in a bowe, which be weaker then other. And for this purpoſe muſt your bowe be well trimmed and pyked of a cunninge man, that it maye come rounde in compaſſe everye where.

[6] Freates.

For

For freates you muſt beware, if your bow have a knot in the backe, leſt the places which be next it, be not alowed ſtronge enoughe to bere with the knot, or els the ſtronge knot ſhall freate the weake places next it. Freates be firſt litle pinches, the which when you perceave, pike the places about the pinches, to make them ſomewhat weaker, and as well comminge as where it pinched, and ſo the pinches ſhall dye, and never encreaſe farther into freates.

Freates begin many times in a pinne, for there the good woode is corrupted, that it muſt nedes be weake, and becauſe it is weake, therefore it freates. Good bowyers therefore do raiſe every pinne, and alowe it more woode for feare of freatinge.

Againe, bowes moſt commonly freate under the hand, not ſo much as ſome men ſuppoſe for the moiſtneſſe of the hand, as for the heate of the hand. The nature of the heat, ſayth *Ariſtotle*, is to looſe, and not to knitte faſt, and the more looſer the more weaker, the more weaker the redier to freate.

A bowe is not well made, which hath not woode plentye in the hande. For if the endes of the
bowe

bowe be ftiffifhe, or a mans hand any thinge hote, the bellye muft nedes fone frete. Remedye for freates to any purpofe I never harde tell of anye, but only to make the freated place as ftrong, or ftronger, than anye other. To fill up the freate with litle fhevers of a quill and glewe, as fome faye will do well, by reafon muft be ftarke nought. For, put the cafe the freate did ceafe then, yet the caufe which made it freate afore, (and that is weakneffe of the place) becaufe it is not taken away, muft needes make it freate againe. As for cuttinge out of freates, with all maner of peecinge of bowes, I will cleane exclude from perfite fhootinge. For peeced bowes be much like ould houfen, which be more chargeable to repayre then commodious to dwell in. And againe, to fwadle a bowe much about with bandes, verye feldome doth anye good, excepte it be to keepe down a fpell in the backe, otherwife bandes eyther nede not, when the bowe is any thing worthe, or els boote not, when it is marde and paft beft. And although I know mean and poore fhooters will ufe peeced and banded bowes fome- times, becaufe they are not able to get better when they would, yet, I am fure, if they would con- fider it well, they fhall find it both leffe charge and more pleafure, to beftowe at any time a couple of

fhillinges

ſhillinges of a newe bowe, than to beſtowe ten
pence of peecing an old bowe. For better is coſte
upon ſomewhat worth, than ſpence upon nothinge worth. And this I ſpeake alſo, becauſe
you would have me referre all to perfiteneſſe in
ſhootinge.

Moreover there is another thinge, which will
ſone cauſe a bowe to be broken by one of the three
wayes which be firſt ſpoken of, and that is ſhootinge
in * Winter, when there is anye froſt. Froſt is
whereſoever is any wateriſhe humour, as is in
woodes, eyther more or leſſe, and you knowe that
all thinges froſen and iſie will rather breake than
bende. Yet, if a man muſt needes ſhoote at any
ſuch time, let him take his bowe and bringe it to
the fire, and there, by little and little, rubbe and
chafe it with a waxed clothe, which ſhall bringe it
to that point, that he maye ſhoote ſafely enough
in it. This rubbing with waxe, as I ſayde before,
is a greate ſuccour againſt all wete and moyſtneſſe.
In the fieldes alſo, in going betwixt the prickes,
eyther with your hand, or els with a cloth, you
muſt kepe your bowe in ſuch a temper.

* Boyle ſomewhere mentions a Pole, who related, that the cold of his
countries winters broke his bow.

And

And thus much as concerninge your bowe, howe firſt to knowe what woode it beſt for a bowe, then to choſe a bowe, after to trimme a bowe, againe to kepe it in goodneſſe, laſt of all, how to ſave it from all harme and evilneſſe. And although many men can ſaye more of a bowe, yet I truſt theſe thinges be true, and almoſt ſufficient for the knowledge of a perfect bowe.

PHI. Surelye I believe ſo, and yet I could have heard you talke longer on it : although I cannot ſee what may be ſayd more of it. Therefore, excepte you will pauſe a while, you may go forwarde to a ſhaft.

TOX. What [7] ſhaftes were made of, in ould time, authours do not ſo manifeſtly ſhewe, as of bowes. [8] *Herodotus* doth tell, that in the floude of *Nilus* there was a beaſte, called a Water Horſe, of whoſe ſkin, after it was dryed, the *Egyptians* made ſhaftes and dartes. The tree called *Cornus* was ſo common to make ſhaftes of, that, in good authors of the *Latine* tongue, *Cornus* is taken for a ſhafte, as in [9] *Seneca*, and that place of *Virgill.*

Volat itala cornus,   Virg. En. 9.

[7] Shaftes. [8] Herod. Euterp. [9] Sen. Hipp.

Yet,

Yet, of all thinges that ever I marked of ould authors, eyther *Greeke* or *Latine*, for fhaftes to be made of, there is nothinge fo common as reedes. *Herodotus*, in defcribinge the mightye hoaft of *Xerxes*, doth tell, that three greate countryes ufed fhaftes made of a rede, the [10] *Ethiopians*, the *Lycians*, (whofe fhaftes lacked fethers, whereat I marveile moft of all) and the men of *Inde*. The fhaftes of *Inde* were very longe, a yarde and an halfe, as [1] *Arrianus* doth faye, or, at the leaft, a yarde, as [2] *Q. Curtius* doth faye, and therefore they gave the greater ftrype, but yet, becaufe they were fo longe, they were the more unhanfome, and leffe profitable to the men of *Inde*, as *Curtius* doth tell.

In *Crete* and *Italy* they ufed to have theyr fhaftes of reede alfo. The beft reede for fhaftes grew in [3] *Inde*, and in *Rhenus*, a floud of *Italye*. But, becaufe fuch fhaftes be neyther eafye for *Englifhemen* to get, and, if they were gotten, fcarce profitable for them to ufe, I will let them paffe, and fpeake of thofe fhaftes which *Englifhemen*, at this daye, moft commonly do approve and allowe. A fhaft hath three principall parts, the ftele, the fethers, and

[10] In Polym.   [1] Arrianus 8.   [2] Q. Curt. 8.   [3] Plin. 16. 36.

Y   the

the head: whereof every one muſt be ſeverallye ſpoken of.

Steles be made of divers woodes: as,

Braſell,	Byrche,	Blackthorne,
Turkie Woode,	Aſſhe,	Beche,
Fuſticke,	Oake,	Elder,
Sugercheſte,	Serviſtree,	Aſpe,
Hardbeame,	Hulder,	Salowe.

Theſe woodes, as they be moſt commonly uſed, ſo they be moſt fit to be uſed: yet ſome one fitter then an other for divers mens ſhootinge, as ſhall be told afterward. And in this pointe, as in a bowe, you muſt truſte an honeſt fletcher. Neverthelesse, although I cannot teach you to make a bowe or a ſhaft, which belongeth to a bowyer and a fletcher to come to theyr lyving, yet will I ſhewe you ſome tokens to know a bowe and a ſhafte, which pertayneth to an archer to come to good ſhootinge.

A ſtele muſt be well * ſeaſoned for caſtinge, and it muſt be made as the graine lyeth, and as it groweth, or els it will never flye cleane, as clothe

---

* Seaſoned for caſtinge, that is, well ſeaſoned to hinder it from warping.

cut

cut overthwart, and againſt the wull, can never hooſe a man cleane. A knotty ſtele may be ſuffered in a bigge ſhaft, but for a little ſhaft it is nothing fit, both becauſe it will never flye farre, and, beſides that, it is ever in danger of breaking, it flyeth not farre becauſe the ſtrength of the ſhoote is hindered and ſtopped at the knot, even as a ſtone caſt into a plaine even ſtill water, will make the water move a great ſpace, yet, if there be any whirlinge plat in the water, the moving ceaſeth when it cometh at the whirling plat, which is not much unlike a knot in a ſhaft, if it be conſidered well. So every thing as it is plaine and ſtraight of his own nature, ſo it is fitteſt for farre movinge. Therefore a ſtele which is harde to ſtand in a bowe withoute knot, and ſtreighte, (I mean not artificiallye ſtreight as the fletcher doth make it, but naturallye ſtreighte as it groweth in the woode) is beſt to make a ſhafte of, eyther to go cleane, flye farre, or ſtande ſurely in anye weather.

Now how bigge, how ſmall, how heavye, how light, how long, how ſhort, a ſhaft ſhould be particularly for every man, ſeeing we muſt talke of the general nature of ſhootinge, can not be toulde no more than you Rhetoricians can appoint anye one kind

kind of wordes, of fentences, of figures, fit for everye matter, but even as the man and the matter reqⁱyreth, fo the fitteſt to be uſed. Therefore, as concerninge thoſe contraryes in a ſhaft, everye man muſt avoyde them, and drawe to the meane of them, which mean is beſt in all thinges. Yet if a man happen to offende in any of the extremes, it is better to offende in want and ſcantneſſe, than in to much and outragious excedinge   As it is better to have a ſhaft a litle to ſhort, than over longe, ſomewhat to light, than over lumpiſhe, a litle to ſmal, than a greate deale to big, which thinge is not only truly ſayde in ſhootinge, but in all other thinges that ever man goeth about, as in eatinge, taulkinge, and all other thinges like, which matter was once excellentlye diſputed upon, in the ſcholes, you know when.

And to offende, in theſe contraryes, commeth much, if men take not heede, throughe the kinde of woode, whereof the ſhaft is made; for ſome woode belonges to that exceedinge part, ſome to the ſcant part, ſome to the meane, as Braſell, Turkie woode, Fuſticke, Sugar cheſte, and ſuch like, make dead, heavye, lump ſhe, hobbling ſhaftes. Againe, Hulder, Blacke thorne, Serveſtree, Beeche, Elder,

Elder, Afpe, and Salowe, eyther for theyr weaknefs or lightneffe, make holow, ftarting, fcudding, gaddinge fhaftes. But Birche, Hardbeame, fome Oake, and fome Afhe, being both ftronge enoughe to ftande in a bowe, and alfo light enoughe to fly farre, are beft for a meane, which is to be fought out in every thinge. And although I know, that fome men fhoote fo ftronge, that the deade woodes be light enough for them, and other fome fo weake, that the loufe woodes be likewyfe for them bigge enoughe, yet generallye, for the moft part of men, the meane is the beft. And fo to conclude, that is alwayes beft for a man, which is meeteft for him. Thus no woode of his owne nature is eyther to light or to heavy, but as the fhooter is himfelfe which doth ufe it. For that fhaft, which one yeare for a man is to lighte and fcuddinge, for the felfe fame reafon the next yeare may chaunce to be heavye and hobblinge. Therefore cannot I expreffe, except generallye, what is beft woode for a fhafte, but let everye man, when he knoweth his owne ftrengthe, and the nature of everye woode, provide and fit himfelfe thereafter. Yet, as concerninge fheaffe arrowes for war, (as I fuppofe) it were better to make them of good Afhe, and not of Afpe, as they be now a dayes. For of all other

woodes

woodes that ever I proved, Afhe beinge bigge is
fwifteft, and againe hevye to geve a great ftripe
withall, which Afpe fhall not do. What heavineffe
doth in a ftripe every man by experience can tell,
therefore Afhe being both * fwifter and heavyer,
is more fit for fheafe arrowes than Afpe, and thus
much for the beft woode for fhaftes.

Againe likewife as no one woode can be greatlye
meete for all kinde of fhaftes, no more can one
fafhion of the ftele be fit for every fhooter. For
thofe that be little breafted and bigge towarde the
heade, called by theyr likeneffe Taper fafhion,
Refhe Growne, and of fome mery felowes Bob-
tailes, be fit for them which fhoote under hand,
becaufe they fhoote with a fofte loufe, and ftreffes
not a fhafte much in the brefte, where the weight
of the bowe lyeth, as you may perceyve by the
weringe of everye fhafte. Againe, the bigge breafted
fhaft is fit for him which fhooteth right afore him,
or els the breaft beinge weake fhould never with-
ftande that ftronge pithye kinde of fhootinge; thus,
the under hand muft have a fmal breft to go clene

---

* This account of the qualities of the afh, which is reprefented as having
fome peculiar power of fwiftnefs, is obfcure. He probably means, that afh is
the wood which, in a quantity proper for an arrow, has weight enough to
ftrike hard, and lightnefs enough to fly far.

away

away out of the bowe, the fore hand muſt have a
bigge breſte to beare the great might of the bowe.
The ſhaft muſt be made rounde, nothing flat,
without gall or wemme, for this purpoſe. For becauſe roundneſſe (whether you take example in
heaven or in earthe) is fitteſt ſhappe and forme
both for faſt movinge, and alſo for ſone percinge of
any thinge. And therefore *Ariſtotle* ſayth, that nature hath made the raine to be rounde, becauſe it
ſhould the eaſelyer enter through the ayre.

The nocke of the ſhaft is diverſely made, for
ſome be great and full, ſome handſome and litle;
ſome wyde, ſome narowe, ſome deepe, ſome ſhalowe, ſome rounde, ſome longe, ſome with one
nocke, ſome with double nocke, whereof every one
hath his propertye. The great and full nocke may
be well felt, and manye wayes they ſave a ſhaft
from breakinge. The handſome and litle nocke
will go cleane awaye from the hand, the wyde nocke
is noughe, both for breakinge of the ſhafte and alſo
for ſodaine ſlippinge out of the ſtringe, when the
narrowe nocke doth avoyde both thoſe harmes. The
deepe and longe nocke is good in warre for ſure
keepinge in of the ſtringe. The ſhalowe and rounde
nocke is beſt for our purpoſe in pricking for cleane
deliverance

deliverance of a fhoote. And double nockinge is ufed for double fuertye of the fhafte. And thus farre as concerninge a hoole fteele. Peecinge of a fhaft with Brafell and Hollie, or other heavye woodes, is to make the ende * compaffe heavye with the feathers in flyinge, for the ftedfafter fhootinge. For if the ende were plumpe heavye with leade and the wood next it light, the head ende would ever be downwards, and never flye ftreight. Two pointes in peecinge be enough, leaft the moyftneffe of the earth enter to much into the peecinge, and fo loufe the glue. Therefore many pointes be more pleafaunte to the eye, than profitable for the ufe. Some ufe to peece theyr fhaftes in the nocke with Brafell or Hollye, to counterwey with the heade, and I have feene fome for the fame purpofe bore an hole a litle beneath the nocke, and put leade in it. But yet none of thefe wayes be any thing needfull at all, for the nature of a feather in flying, if a man mark it well, is able to beare uppe a wonderful weight: and I thincke fuch peecinge came uppe firft, thus: when a good archer hath broken a good fhaft, in the feathers, and for the fantafie he hath had to it, he is loth to leefe it, and therefore doth he peece it. And then by and by

* Compaffe heavye, feems to fignify proportionately heavy.

other,

other, either becaufe it is gaye, or els becaufe they
will have a fhaft like a good archer, cutteth theyr
hole fhaftes, and peeceth them againe : a thinge,
by my judgmente, more coftlye than nedefull.
And thus have you hearde what woode, what fafhion, what nockinge, what peecinge, a ftele muft
have. Now foloweth the featheringe.

PHI. I would never have thought you could
have fayde half fo much of a ftele, and, I thincke,
as concerninge the litle feather, and the playne
heade, there is but litle to faye.   Tox. Litle,
Yes, truly : for there is no one thinge in all fhoot-
tinge fo much to be looked on as the feather.   For,
firft, a queftion may he afked : Whether any other
thinge befyde a feather, be fit for a fhaft or no ?
If a feather only be fit, whether a goofe feather
onlye or no ? If a goofe feather be beft, then
whether there be any difference as concerninge the
feather of an olde goofe, and a younge goofe ; a
gander, or a goofe ; a fenny goofe, or an upland-
ifhe goofe ?   Againe, which is the beft feather in
any goofe, the right winge or the left winge, the
pinion feather, or any other feather : a whyte,
blacke, or greye feather ? Thirdly, in fetting on
your feather, whether it is pared or drawn with a
Z   thicke

thicke rybbe, or a thinne rybbe, (the rybbe is the hard quill which divideth the feather) a long feather better or a shorte, set on near the nocke, or far from the nocke, set on streight, or somewhat bowinge? And whether one or two feathers runne on the bowe. Fourthlye, in coulinge or sheeringe, whether highe or lowe, whether somewhat swyne backed (I must use shooters wordes) or sadle backed, whether rounde or square shorne? And whether a shaft at any time ought to be plucked, and howe to be plucked?

PHI. Surely, *Toxophile*, I thincke many fletchers, although daylye they have these thinges in ure, if they were asked sodenly, what they could say of a fether, they could not saye so much. But I pray you let me heare you more at large expresse those thinges in a feather, the which you packed up in so narrowe a roume. And first, whether any other thing may be used for a feather or not. TOX. That was the first pointe indede, and because there foloweth many after, I will hye apace over them, as one that had many a mile to ryde. Shaftes to have had alwayes feathers, [4] *Plinius* in *Latine*, and [5] *Julius Pollux* in *Greke*, do plainlye shewe, yet

[4] Plin. 16. 36. [5] J. Pol. 1. 10.

onlye

onlye the *Lycians* I reade in [6] *Herodotus*, to have
ufed fhaftes without feathers.   Onelye a feather is
fit for a fhaft for two caufes, firft becaufe it is
* leath, weake to geve place to the bowe, then
becaufe it is of that nature, that it will ftarte up
after the bowe.   So plate, woode, or horne, cannot ferve, becaufe they will not geve place.   Againe,
clothe, paper, or parchmente, cannot ferve, becaufe they will not ryfe after the bowe, therefore a
feather is only meete, becaufe it only will do both.
Nowe to loke on the feathers of all maner of
byrdes, you fhall fee fome fo lowe, weake and
fhort, fome fo courfe, ftore and harde, and the
ribbe fo brickle, thin and narrow, that it can neither
be drawen, pared, nor yet well fet on, that excepte
it be a fwanne for a deade fhaft, (as I knowe fome
good archers have ufed) or a ducke for a flight,
which laftes but one fhoote, there is no feather but
onlye of a goofe that hath all commodities in it.
And trulye at a fhorte butte, which fome man doth
ufe, the peacock feather doth feldome kepe up the
fhaft eyther right or level, it is fo rough and heavye,
fo that manye men, which have taken them up for
gayneffe, hath layde them down agayne for profite,

[6] Herod. Pol.

* Leath is limber, flexible, eafily giving way.   Milton calls it lithe.

thus,

thus, for our purpofe, the goofe is the beft feather, for the beft fhooter. PHI. No that is not fo, for the beft fhooter that ever was, ufed other feathers. Tox. Yea, are you fo cunninge in fhootinge? I praye you who was that? PHI. *Hercules*, which had his fhaftes feathered with eagles feathers, as [7] *Hefiodus* doth fay. Tox. Well, as for *Hercules*, feeing neyther water nor lande, heaven nor hell, coulde fcarce content him to abyde in, it was no marveile though felye poore goofe feather coulde not pleafe him to fhoote withal; and againe, as for eagles, they flye fo hye and builde fo farre of, that they be very harde to come by. Yet well fare the gentle [8] goofe, which bringeth to a man, even to his doore, fo manye exceeding commodities. For the goofe is mans comfort in warre and in peace, fleepinge and wakinge. What prayfe foever is geven to fhootinge, the goofe may challenge the beft part in it. Howe well dothe fhe make a man fare at his table? Howe eafilye dothe fhe make a man lye in his bedde? Howe fit even as her feathers be only for fhootinge, fo be her quills fit only for writinge. PHI. Indede, *Toxophile*, that is the beft prayfe you gave to a goofe yet, and

[7] Hefiodus in Seuto. Her. [8] A Goofe.

furely

surely I would have sayde you had bene to blame, if you had overskipte it.

Tox. The *Romaynes*, I trowe, *Philologe*, not so much because a goose with crying saved their *Capitolium*, and heade toure, with their golden *Jupiter*, as *Propertius* doth say very pretely in this verse,

Anseris et tutum voce fuisse Jovem.　　　　Propertius.
Id est,
Theves on a night had stolne Jupiter, had a goose not a kekede.

Did make a golden [9] goose, and set her in the toppe of the *Capitolium*, and appointed also the *Censores* to allow out of the common butche yearely stipendes, for the findinge of certaine geese; the *Romaynes*, did not, I saye, geeve all this honour to a goose for that good dede onely, but for other infinite mo, which come daily to a man by geese; and surelye if I should declame in the prayse of any maner of best lyvinge, I would chuse a goose. But the goose hath made us flee to farre from our matter. Now, Sir, ye have heard how a feather must be had, and that a goose feather onlye: it foloweth of a young goose and an olde, and the residue belonginge to a feather: which thinge I will shortlye course over; whereof, when you knowe the pro-

[9] Livius 1. Dec. 5.

perties,

perties, you may fit your fhaftes according to your
fhootinge, which rule you muft obferve in all other
thinges to, becaufe no one fafhion or quantitye can
be fit for every man, no more than a fhooe or a
cote can be. The olde goofe feather is ftiffe and
ftronge, good for a wynde, and fitteft for a dead
fhâft: the younge goofe feather is weake and fyne,
beft for a fwifte fhafte, and it muft be couled at the
firft fheeringe, fomewhat hye, for with fhootinge it
will fattle and faule very much. The fame thing
(althoughe not fo much) is to be confidered in a
goofe and a gander. A fenny goofe, even as
her flefhe is blacker, ftoorer, unholfomer, fo is
her feather, for the fame caufe, courfer, ftoorer,
and rougher, and therefore I have heard very good
fletchers fay, that the fecond fether in fome place
is better than the pinion in other fome. Betwixt
the winges is litle difference, but that you muft
have divers fhaftes of one flight, feathered with divers
winges, for divers wyndes: for if the wynd and
the feather go both one waye, the fhafte will be
caryed to much. The pinion feathers, as it hath
the firft place in the winge, fo it hath the firft place in
good featheringe. You may know it afore it be
pared, by a bought which is in it, and againe when
it is couled, by the thicknefle above, and the thicknefle

neffe at the grounde, and alfo by the ftiffneffe and finefe which will cary a fhaft better, fafter and further, even as a fine fayle cloth doth a fhippe.

The coloure of the feather is leaft to be regarded, yet fomewhat to be loked on ; for a good white you have fometimes an ill greye. Yet furely it ftandeth with good reafon, to have the cocke feather blacke or greye, as it were to geve a man warninge to nocke right. The cocke feather is called that which ftandeth above in right nockinge, which if you do not obferve, the other feathers muft needes runne on the bowe, and fo marre your fhote. And thus farre of the goodneffe and choyce of your feather : now foloweth the fetting on. Wherein you muft looke that your feathers be not drawen for haftineffe, but pared even and ftreight with diligence. The fletcher draweth a feather when it hath but one fwappe at it with his knife, and then playneth it a litle, with rubbing it over his knife. He pareth it when he taketh leyfure and heede, to make everye part of the rybbe apt to ftand ftreight and even on upon the ftele. This thing, if a man take not hede on, he may chaunce have caufe to fay fo of his fletcher, as in dreffinge of meate is commonlye fayde of cookes : and that is, that God fendeth us

good

good feathers, but the devill noughtye fletchers.
If anye fletchers heard me fay thus, they would not
be angrye with me, excepte they were ill fletchers :
and yet by reafon, thofe fletchers too ought rather
to amende themfelves for doing ill, than be angrye
with me for faying truth. The ribbe in a ftiffe
feather may be thinner, for fo it will ftande
cleaner on : but in a weake feather you muft
leave a thicker ribbe, or els if the ribbe, which
is the foundation and grounde wherein nature hath
fet every clefte of the feather, be taken to nere the
feather, it muft nedes folow, that the feather fhall
fall and droup down, even as any herbe doth which
hath his roote to nere taken on with a fpade. The
length and fhortneffe of the feather ferveth for
divers fhaftes, as a longe feather for a longe, heavye,
or byg fhafte, the fhort feather for the contrarye.
Againe, the fhorte maye ftande farther, the longe
nerer the nocke. Your feather muft ftand almoft
ftreight on, but yet after that fort, that it may turne
rounde in flyinge.

And here I confider the wonderfull nature of
fhootinge, which ftandeth altogether by that fafhion, which is moft apt for quicke movinge, and
that is by roundneffe. For firft the bowe muft be
gathered

gathered rounde, in drawinge it muſt come rounde compaſſe, the ſtringe muſt be rounde, the ſtele muſt be round, the beſt nocke rounde, the feather ſhorne ſomewhat rounde, the ſhaft in flyinge muſt turne rounde, and, if it flye far, it flyeth a rounde compaſſe, for eyther above or beneathe a rounde compaſſe hindereth the flyinge. Moreover, both the fletcher in makinge your ſhaft, and you in nockinge your ſhaft, muſt take heede that two feathers equally runne on the bow. For if one feather runne alone on the bowe, it ſhall quickely be worne, and ſhall not be able to match with the other feathers ; and againe, at the lowſe, if the ſhaft be light, it will ſtart, if it be heavye, it will hoble. And thus as concerning ſettinge on of your feather. Now of coulinge.

To ſhere a ſhaft highe or lowe, muſt be as the ſhafte is, heavye or light, great or litle, long or ſhort, the ſwyne backed faſhion maketh the ſhaft deader, for it gathereth more ayre than the ſaddle backed, and therefore the ſaddle backe is ſurer for daunger of weather, and fitter for ſmothe flyinge. Againe, to ſhere a ſhaft rounde, as they were wont ſometimes to do, or after the tryangle faſhion, which is muche uſed now a dayes, both be good. For

A a   roundneſſe

roundneffe is apte for flyinge of his own nature, and all maner of tryangle fafhion (the fharpe pointe goinge before) is alfo naturallye apte for quicke entringe; and therefore fayth [10] *Cicero*, that cranes, taught by nature, obferve in flyinge a tryangle fafhion alwayes, becaufe it is fo apte to perce and go through the ayre withall. Laft of all, pluckinge of feathers is nought, for there is no furetye in it, therefore let every archer have fuch fhaftes, that he may both know them and truft them at every chaunge of weather. Yet, if they muft nedes be plucked, plucke them as litle as can be, for fo fhall they be the leffe unconftant. And thus I have knit up in as fhort a roume as I could, the beft feathers, featheringe, and coulinge of a fhaft.

PHI. I thincke furelye you have fo taken up the matter with you, that you have left nothinge behinde you. Nowe you have broughte a fhafte to the heade, which, if it were on, we had done as concerninge all inftrumentes belonging to fhootinge.   TOX. Neceffitye, the inventor of all goodneffe (as all authors in a manner do faye) amonges all other thinges invented a fhaft head, firft to fave the end from breakinge, then it made

[10] De Nat. Deor.

it

it ſharpe it ſticke better, after it made it of ſtrong
matter, to laſt better: laſt of all, experience and wyſedome of men hath brought it to ſuch a perfitneſſe,
that there is no one thinge ſo profitable belonging to
artillerye, either to ſtrike a mans enemye ſorer in
warre, or to ſhoote nerer the marke at home, than is a
fitte heade for both purpoſes. For if a ſhaft lacke
a heade, it is worth nothing for neyther uſe.
Therefore, ſeeinge heades be ſo neceſſarye, they
muſt of neceſſitye be well loked upon. Heades for
warre, of longe time hath bene made, not onlye of
divers matters, but alſo of divers faſhions. The
Troyans had heades of yron, as this verſe, ſpoken of
Pandarus, ſheweth :

Up to the pappe his ſtringe did he pull, his ſhaft to the harde yron. Iliad 4.

The *Grecians* had heades of braſſe, as *Ulyſſes*
ſhaftes were headed, when he ſlewe *Antonius* and
the other wowers of *Penelope*.

----Quite throughe a dore ſlewe a ſhaft with a braſſe head. Odyſſ. 21.

It is playne in [1] *Homer*, where *Menelaus* was
wounded of *Pandarus* ſhaftes, that the heades were
not glewed on, but tyed on with a ſtring, as the

[1] Iliad. 4.

A a 2　　　　　commentaryes

commentaryes in *Greke* plainly tell. And therefore
shooters, at that time, used to carye theyr shaftes
without heades, until they occupyed them, and
then set on an head, as it appeareth in *Homer*, the
twenty-first booke *Odyssey*, where *Penelope* brought
Ulysses bow downe amonges the gentlemen which
came on wowing to her, that he which was able to
bende it and drawe it, might enjoy her, and after
her folowed a mayde, sayth [2] *Homer*, caryinge a
bagge full of heades, both of yron and brasse.

The men of *Scythia* used heads of brasse. The
men of *Inde* used heads of yron. The *Ethiopians*
used heads of hard sharpe stone, as both [3] *Herodotus*
and *Pollux* doth tell. The *Germaines*, as *Cornelius
Tacitus* doth saye, had theyr shaftes headed with
bone, and manye countryes, both of olde time and
nowe, use heades of horne. But, of all other, yron
and stele must nedes be the fittest for heades.
[4] *Julius Pollux* calleth otherwyse than we do, where
the feathers be the heade, and that which we call
the heade, he calleth the point.

Fashion of heades is divers, and that of olde time:
two manner of arrowes heades, sayth *Pollux*, was

[2] Odyss. 21. [3] Herod. Clio. Polym. [4] J. Pol. 1. 10.

used

ufed in olde time. The one he calleth ὄγκινος deſcribinge it thus, havinge two pointes or barbes, lokinge backeward to the ſtele and the feathers, which ſurelye we call in *Engliſhe* a brode arrowe head, or a ſwalowe tayle. The other he calleth γλῶχις, having two pointes ſtretchinge forwarde, and this *Engliſhemen* do call a forke heade: both theſe two kindes of heades were uſed in *Homers* dayes, for *Teucer* uſed forked heades, ſayinge thus to *Agamemnon*,

Eight good ſhaftes have I ſhot ſith I came, ech one with a forke heade. Iliad. 8.

Pandarus heades and *Ulyſſes* heades were brode arrowe heades, as a man maye learne in *Homer*, that would be curious in knowinge that matter. *Hercules* uſed forked heades, but yet they had three pointes or forkes, when other mens had but two. The *Parthians* at that great battaile where they ſlue riche *Craſſus* and his ſonne, uſed brode arrowe heades, whiche ſtacke ſo ſore that the [5] *Romaynes* could not pull them out againe. *Commodus* the Emperour uſed forked heades, whoſe faſhion [6] *Herodian* doth lively and naturallye deſcribe, ſayinge, that they were like the ſhap of a newe mone, wherewith he woulde ſmite the head of a birde, and never

[5] Plutarchus in Craſſo.   [6] Herod. 1.

miſſe;

miſſe; other faſhion of heades have not I redde
on. Our *Engliſhe* heades be better in warre than
eyther forked heades or brode arrowe heades. For
firſt, the ende beinge lighter, they flee a great deale
the faſter, and, by the ſame reaſon, geveth a farre
ſorer ſtripe. Yea, and, I ſuppoſe, if the ſame litle
barbes which they have, were clean put awaye,
they ſhould be farre better. For this every man
doth graunt, that a ſhaft, as long as it flyeth,
* turnes, and when it leaveth turning, it leaveth
going any farther. And every thing that enters
by a turninge and boringe faſhion, the more flatter
it is, the worſe it enters, as a knife, though it be
ſharpe, yet, becauſe of the edges, will not bore ſo
well as a bodkin, for everye rounde thinge enters
beſt; and therefore nature, ſayth *Ariſtotle*, made
the raine droppes round, for quicke percinge the
ayre. Thus, eyther ſhaftes turne not in flyinge,
or elſe our flat arrow heades ſtop the ſhaft in en-
tering.   PHI. But yet, *Toxophile*, to hold your
communication a litle, I ſuppoſe the flat head is
better, both becauſe it maketh a greater hole, and
alſo becauſe it ſtickes faſter in.   Tox. Theſe

---

* If it be true, as we believe it is, that a ſhaft turns round in flying, it is not
true that triangular ſhafts are good for piercing, as has been ſaid by the author, nor that Commodus could intercept the neck of a bird between the
two points of a half moon.

two reasons, as they be both true, so they be both nought. For first, the lesse hole, if it be deepe, is the worse to heale againe: when a man shooteth at his enemy he desyreth rather that it should enter farre than sticke fast. For what remedye is it, I praye you, for him that is smitten with a deepe wounde, to pull out the shaft quicklye, except it be to hast his death spedelye? Thus heades which make a litle hole and deep, be better in warre, than those which make a great hole and sticke fast in. [7] *Julius Pollux* maketh mention of certaine kindes of heades for warre, which beare fyre in them, and [8] Scripture also speaketh somewhat of the same. [9] *Herodotus* doth tell a wonderfull policy to be done by *Xerxes*, what time he besieged the great tower in *Athens:* He made his archers binde theyr shaft heades about with towe, and then set it on fyre and shoote them, which thing done by many archers, set all the place on fyre, which were of matter to burne: and, besydes that, dased the men within, so that they knew not whyther to turne them. But, to make an end of all heades for warre, I woulde wyshe that the heade makers of *Englande* should make theyr sheafe arrow heades more harder pointed than they be: for I myselfe have seene of late such

[7] Pollux 7.   [8] Psalm 7.   [9] Herod. Vran.

heades

heades set upon sheafe arrowes, as the officers, if they had seene them, would not have bene content withall.

Nowe as concerninge heades for prickinge, which is our purpose, there be divers kindes, some be blont heades, some sharpe, some both blonte and sharpe. The blonte heades men use, because they perceive them to be good to kepe a lengthe withall, they kepe a good lengthe, because a man pulleth them no further at one time than at another; for in feelinge the plompe ende always equallye, he may lowse them. Yet, in a winde, and againſt the winde, the weather hath so much power on the brode ende, that no man can kepe no sure length with such a head; therefore a blont head, in a caulme or downe a winde, is very good, otherwise none worse. Sharpe heades at the ende, without any shoulders, (I call that the shoul-ders in a heade which a mans finger shall feele afore it come to the point) will perch quicklye through a winde, but yet it hath two discommo-dities, the one that it will kepe no length, it kepeth no length, because no man can pull it, certainly as farre at one time as at another : it is not drawen certainly so farre one time as at another, because it

lacketh

lacketh fhoulderinge, wherewith, as with a fure token, a man might be warned when to loufe ; and alfo becaufe men are afrayd of the fharpe pointe for fettinge it in the bowe. The fecond incommoditye is when it is lighted on the grounde, the fmall point fhall everye time be in jeopardye of hurtinge, which thinge, of all other, will foneft make the fhaft lefe the length. Nowe, when blont heades be good to kepe a length withall, yet nought for a winde ; fharpe heades good to perch the weather withal, yet nought for a length ; certaine heade makers, dwellinge in *London*, perceyving the commoditye of both kindes of heades, joyned with a difcommoditye, invented new files and other in-ftrumentes, wherewith they brought heades for prickinge to fuch a perfitneffe, that all the commodityes of the two other heades fhould be put in one heade, without any difcommodity at all. They made a certaine kinde of heades, which men call Hie Rigged, Creafed, or Shouldred heades, or Silver-fpoon heades, for a certaine likeneffe that fuch heades have with the knob ende of fome filver fpones. Thefe heades be good both to kepe a length withall, and alfo to perche a winde withall. To kepe a length withall, becaufe a man maye certainly pull it to the fhoulderinge every

B b   fhoote,

shoote, and no farther; to perch a winde withall, becaufe the point, from the fhoulder forward, breaketh the weather as all other fharpe thinges doo. So the blont fhoulder ferveth for a fure length kepinge, the pointe alfo is ever fit for a roughe and great weather percinge. And thus much, as fhortly as I could, as concerninge heades both for warre and peace. PHI. But is there no cunninge as concerninge fetting on of the heade. TOX. Well remembred. But that point belong-eth to fletchers, yet you may defyre him to fet your heade full on, and clofe on. Full on is when the woode is bet harde up to the ende or ftoppinge of the heade; clofe on, is when there is left woode on everye fyde the fhafte, enoughe to fill the head withall, or when it is neyther too litle nor yet too great. If there be anye fault in any of thefe pointes, the heade, when it lighteth on an harde ftone, or grounde, will be in jeopardye, eyther of breakinge, or els otherwife hurtinge. Stopping of heades eyther with leade or any thinge els, fhall not nede nowe, becaufe every filver fpoone, or fhouldred heade, is ftopped of itfelfe. Shorte heades be better than longe: for firft, the longe heade is worfe for the maker to file ftreight com-paffe everye waye; againe, it is worfe for the fletcher

to

to fet ftraight on; thirdlye, it is alwayes in more jeopardye of breakinge when it is on. And now, I trowe, *Philologe*, we have done as concerninge all inftrumentes belonging to fhootinge, which every fere archer ought to provide for himfelfe. And there remayneth two thinges behinde, which be general or common to every man, the weather and the marke, but, becaufe they be fo knit with fhootinge ftraighte, or kepinge of a lengthe, I will refer them to that place; and now we will come (God willinge) to handle our inftrumentes, the thinge that every man defyreth to do well. PHI. If you teache me fo well to handle the inftrumentes as you have defcrybed them, I fuppofe I fhall be an archer good enoughe. TOX. To learne any thinge, (as you know better than I, *Philologe*) and efpeciallye to do a thinge with a mans handes, muft be done, if a man would be excellent, in his youthe. Younge trees in gardens, which lacke all fenfes, and beaftes without reafon, when they be younge, may, with handlinge and teachinge, be brought to wonderfull thinges.

And this is not onlye true in natural thinges, but in artificiall thinges to, as the potter moft cunningly doth caft his pottes when his claye is foft

B b 2   and

and workable, and waxe taketh print when it is warme, and leathie weake, not when clay and waxe be harde and olde: and even so, every man in his youth, both with witte and bodye, is most apte and pliable to receive any cunning that should be taught him.

This communication of teachinge youth, maketh me remember the right worshipful, and my singular good maister, Sir *Humphreye Wingfielde*, to whom, next God, I ought to referre, for his manifold benefits bestowed on me, the pore talent of learninge which God hath lent me: and for his sake do I owe my service to all other of the name and noble house of the *Wingfieldes*, both in worde and deede. This worshipful man hath ever loved and used to have many children brought up in learninge in his house, amonges whom I myselfe was one. For whom at terme-times he would bringe down from *London* both bowe and shaftes, and, when they should playe, he would go with them himselfe into the fielde, and see them shoote, and he that shotte fayrest, should have the best bowe and shaftes, and he that shotte ill favouredly, should be mocked of his fellowes, till he shotte better.

Would

Would to God all *Englande* had ufed, or would ufe to laye the foundation, after the example of this worfhipful man, in bringinge up children in the booke and the bowe : by which two thinges the hole common wealthe, both in peace and warre, is chieflye ruled and defended withall.

But to our purpofe, he that muft come to this high perfectnefs in fhootinge, which we fpeake of, muft nedes beginne to learne it in his youthe, the omittinge of which thinge in *England*, both maketh fewer fhooters, and alfo every man, that is a fhooter, fhoote worfe than he might if he were taught. PHI. Even as I knowe this is true, which you faye, even fo, *Toxophile*, you have quite difcouraged me, and drawen my minde cleane from fhootinge, feeinge, by this reafon, no man that hath not ufed it in his youthe, can be excellent in it. And I fuppofe the fame reafon would difcourage many other mo, if they heard you talk after this fort. TOX. This thinge, *Philologe*, fhall difcourage no man that is wyfe. For I will prove that wyfedome may worke the fame thinge in a man, that nature doth in a childe.

A childe by three thinges is broughte to excellencye. By aptnefle, defyre, and feare : aptnefle maketh

maketh him pliable, like waxe, to be formed and
fashioned, even as a man would have him. Desyre, to be as good, or better, than his fellowes:
and fear of them whom he is under, will cause him
take great laboure and paine with diligente heede, in
learninge any thing, whereof proceedeth, at the
last, excellencye and perfectnesse.

A man maye, by wysedome in learninge of any
thinge, and speciallye to shoote, have three like
commodityes also, whereby he may, as it were,
become yonge againe, and so attaine to excellencye. For as a childe is apt by naturall youthe, so
a man, by usinge at the first weake bowes, farre
underneth his strength, shall be as pliable and redye
to be taughte fayre shootinge as any childe : and
dailye use of the same shall both keepe him in
fayre shootinge, and also at the last bringe him to
stronge shootinge.

And, instede of the fervent desyre which provoketh a child to be better than his felowe, let a
man be as much stirred up with shamefastnes to be
worse than all other. And the same place that
feare hath in a childe, to compel him to take paine,
the same hath love of shootinge in a man, to cause
him

him forfake no labour, without which nô man nor childe can be excellent. And thus, whatfoever a childe may be taught by aptneffe, defyre, and fear, the fame thinge in fhootinge may a man be taught by weake bowes, fhamefaftneffe and love.

And hereby you may fee that that is true which *Cicero* fayth, that a man, by ufe, may be brought to a newe nature. And this I dare be bould to faye, that anye man which will wifelye beginne, and conftantly perfevere in his trade of learninge to fhoote, fhall attaine to perfectneffe therein. PHI. This communication, *Toxophile*, doth pleafe me very well, and now I perceive that moft generally and chiefly youthe muft be taught to fhoote, and, fecondarilye, no man is debarred therefrom except it be more throughe his own negligence, for becaufe he will not learne, than any difabilitye becaufe he cannot learne. Therefore, feeinge I will be glad to folowe your counfel in chofinge my bowe and other inftrumentes, and alfo am afhamed that I can fhoote no better than I can, moreover, havinge fuch a love towarde fhootinge by your good reafons to daye, that I will forfake no laboure in the exercife of the fame, I befeech you imagine that we had both bow and fhaftes here, and teache me

how

how I fhould handle them ; and one thinge I defyre you, make me as fayre an archer as you can.

For this I am fure, in learninge all other matters, nothing is brought to the moft profitable ufe,
which is not handled after the moft comelye fafhion. As maifters of fence have no ftroke fitte
eyther to hitte an other, or els to defende himfelfe,
which is not joyned with a wonderfull comlineffe.
A cooke cannot choppe his herbes neyther quickely
nor handfomely, excepte he kepe fuch a meafure
mith his choppinge knyves, as would delight a man
both to fee him and heare him. Every handye
crafteman that workes befte for his owne profite,
workes moft femely to other mens fighte. Agayne
in buildinge a houfe, in makinge a fhippe, every
parte, the more hanfomlye they be joyned for
* profite and lafte, the more comelye they be fa-
fhioned to every mans fight and eye.

Nature itfelfe taught men to joyne always well-
favourednefle with profitableneffe. As in man,
that joynte or piece which is by any chaunce de-
prived of his comlineffe, the fame is alfo debarred
of his ufe and profitableneffe. And he that is gogle

* Profite and lafte, convenience and duration.

eyde,

eyde, and lokes a squinte, hath both his countenaunce clene marred, and his fight fore blemifhed,
and fo in all other members like. Moreover, what
time of the year bringeth moft profite with it for
mans ufe, the fame alfo covereth and decketh both
earth and trees with moft comlineffe for mans pleafure. And that time which taketh away the pleafure of the grounde, caryeth with him alfo the profite of the grounde, as every man by experience
knoweth in harde and roughe winters. Some
thinges there be which hath no other ende, but
only comlineffe, as payntinge and dauncing. And
vertue itfelfe is nothinge elfe but comlineffe, as all
Philofophers do agree in opinion; therefore, feeinge
that which is beft done in any matters, is alwayes
moft comlye done, as both *Plato* and *Cicero* in
many places do prove, daily experience doth teache
in other thinges, I praye you, as I faid before,
teache me to fhoote as fayre, wellfavouredly, as you
can ymagen. Tox. Trulye, *Philologe*, as you
prove very well in other matters, the beft fhootinge
is alwayes the moft comlye fhootinge; but this you
know as well as I, that *Craffus* fheweth in *Cicero*,
that, as comlyneffe is the chiefe pointe, and moft
to be fought for in all thinges, fo comlyneffe only
can never be taughte by any arte or craft; but may

C c   be

be perceyved well when it is done, not defcribed
well how it fhould be done. Yet, neverthe-
leffe, to come to it there be many wayes, which
wyfe men hath affayed in other matters, as if a man
would folowe, in learninge to fhoote fayre, the
noble paynter *Zeuxes* in paynting *Helena*, which,
to make his image beautiful, did chofe out five of
the faireft maydes in all the countrye about, and,
in beholdinge them, conceyved and drue out fuch
an image, that it farre exceeded all other, becaufe
the comlineffe of them all was brought into one
moft perfit comlineffe : fo likewyfe in fhootinge, if
a man would fet before his eyes five or fix of the
faireft archers that ever he faw fhoote, and of one
learne to ftande, of another to drawe, of another
to lowfe, and fo take of every man what every man
could do beft ; I dare faye, he fhould come to fuch
a comlineffe as never man came to yet.

PHI. This is very well trulye, but I pray you
teache me fomewhat of fhooting fayre yourfelfe.
TOX. I can teache you to fhoote fayre, even as
Socrates taughte a man ones to know God ; for,
when he afked him what was God, Nay, fayth he,
I can tell you better what God is not, as God is
not ill, God is unfpeakable, unfearchable, and fo
forth ;

forth: even likewyſe can I ſay of fayre ſhootinge, It hath not this diſcommodity with it nor that diſcommodity; and, at laſt, a man may ſo ſhift all the diſcommoditytes from ſhootinge, that there ſhall be left nothinge behinde but fayre ſhootinge. And to do this the better, you muſt remember how that I toulde you, when I deſcrybed generallye the hole nature of ſhootinge, that fayre ſhootinge came of theſe thinges, of ſtandinge, nockinge, drawinge, houldinge, and lowſinge, the which I will go over as ſhortly as I can, deſcribinge the diſcommodities that men commonly uſe in all partes of theyr bodyes, that you, if you faulte in anye ſuch, may know it, and ſo go about to amende it. Faultes in archers do exceed the nomber of archers, which come with uſe of ſhootinge withoute teachinge. Uſe and cuſtome ſeperated from knowledge and learninge, doth not only hurt ſhootinge, but the moſt weightye thinges in the world beſyde: and, therefore, I marveile much at thoſe people which be the maintayners of uſes without knowledge, having no other worde in theyr mouth but this *uſe, uſe, cuſtome, cuſtome.* Such men, more wilfull than wyſe, beſyde other diſcommoditytes, take all place and occaſion from all amendment. And this I ſpeake generallye of uſe and cuſtome. Which

C c 2

thinge,

thinge, if a learned man had it in hand that would applye it to any one matter, he might handle it wonderfully. But, as for shooting, use is the only cause of all faultes in it, and therefore children, more easely and sooner, may be taught to shoote excellently than men, because children may be taught to shoote well at the first, men have more pain to unlearne theyr ill uses, than they have labour afterwarde to come to good shootinge.

All the discommodityes which ill custome hath graffed in archers, can neyther be quickly pulled oute, nor yet soone reckoned of me, there be so many. Some shooteth his head forwarde, as though he would byte the marke; another stareth with his eyes, as though they should flye out; another winketh with one eye and loketh with the other; some make a face with wrything theyr mouth and countenaunce so, as though they were doinge you wotte what; another blereth oute his tongue; another byteth his lippes; another holdeth his necke awrye. In drawinge, some set such a compasse, as though they would turne about, and * blesse all the field; other heave theyr hand now

---

* This alludes to the actions of the Romish priest in public benedictions. This passage may explain a very obscure phrase in Spenser, who calls waving the sword in circles, blessing the sword.

up

up now downe, that a man cannot decerne whereat
they would fhoote : another waggeth the upper end
of his bow one way, the nether ende another way.
Another will ftand pointing his fhaft at the marke
a good while, and, by and by, he will geve him a
whippe, and away or a man witte. Another maketh fuch a wreftlinge with his gere, as thoughe he
were able to fhoote no more as longe as he lived.
Another draweth foftlye to the middes, and, by and
by, it is gone you cannot know howe. Another
draweth his fhaft lowe at the breaft, as thoughe he
would fhoote at a roving marke, and, by and by,
he lifteth his arme up pricke heyght. Another
maketh a wrynchinge with his backe, as thoughe
a man pinched him behinde. Another coureth
downe, and layeth out his buttockes, as thoughe
he fhould fhoote at crowes. Another fetteth forwarde his left legge, and draweth back with heade
and fhoulders, as thoughe he pulled at a rope, or
elfe were afrayed of the mark. Another draweth
his fhaft well, untill within two fingers of the heade,
and then he ftayeth a little, to loke at his marke,
and, that done, pulleth it up to the head, and
lowfeth : which waye, although fome excellent
fhooters do ufe, yet furelye it is a fault, and good
mennes faultes are not to be folowed. Some drawe

to

to farre, some to short, some to slowlye, some to quicklye, some hold over longe, some let go over sone. Some sette theyr shafte on the grounde, and fetcheth him upwarde; another pointeth up towarde the skye, and so bringeth him downwardes.

Ones I sawe a man which used a bracer on his cheke, or else he had scratched all the skinne of the one syde of his face with his drawinge-hande. Another I saw, which, at every shote, after the loose, lifted up his righte legge so far that he was ever in jeopardye of faulinge. Some stampe forwarde, and some leape backward. All these faultes be eyther in the drawinge, or at the loose; with many other mo, which you may easelye perceyve, and so go about to avoyde them.

Now afterward, when the shaft is gone, men have many faultes, which evill custome hath brought them to, and speciallye in cryinge after the shaft, and speaking wordes scarce honest for such an honest pastime.

Such wordes be very tokens of an ill minde, and manifest signes of a man that is subject to inmesurable affections. Good mennes eares do abhorre them,

them, and an honeſt man therefore will avoyde them. And beſydes thoſe which muſt needes have theyr tongue thus walkinge, other men uſe other faultes, as ſome will take theyr bowe and wrythe and wrinche it, to pull in his ſhaft, when it flyeth wyde, as if he drave a cart. Some will geve two or three ſtrydes forwarde, daunſinge and hoppinge after his ſhaft, as longe as it flyeth, as though he were a madde man. Some, which feare to be to farre gone, runne backwarde, as it were to pull his ſhafte backe. Another runneth forwarde, when he feareth to be ſhorte, heavinge after his armes, as thoughe he woulde helpe his ſhafte to flye. Another wrythes, or runneth aſyde, to pull in his ſhafte ſtraight. One lifteth up his heele, and ſo holdeth his foote ſtill, as longe as his ſhafte flyeth. Another caſteth his arme backwarde after the louſe. And another ſwynges his bowe about him, as it were a man with a ſhafte to make roume in a game place. And manye other faultes there be, which now come not to my remembraunce. Thus, as you have hearde, many archers, with marringe theyr face and countenaunce, with other partes of theyr bodye, as it were men that ſhould daunce antiques, be farre from the comely porte in ſhoot-inge, which he that would be excellent muſt loke for.

Of

Of these faultes I have very many myselfe, but I talke not of my shootinge, but of the general nature of shootinge. Now ymagen an archer that is cleane without all these faultes, and I am sure every man would be delighted to see him shoote.

And althoughe such a perfite comlynesse cannot be expressed with any precepte of teachinge, as *Cicero* and other learned men do say, yet I will speake (according to my little knowledge) that thing in it, which if you folowe, although you shall not be without faulte, yet your faulte shall neyther quickly be perceyved, nor yet greatly rebuked of them that stand by. Standing, nocking, drawing, holding, lowsing, done as they should be done, make fayre shootinge.

The first point is when a man should shoote, to take such [10] footinge and standinge, as shall be both comely to the eye, and profitable to his use, setting his countenaunce and all the other partes of his bodye after such a behaviour, and port, that both all his strength may be employed to his own most advantage, and his shote made and handled to other mens pleasure and delyte. A man must

[10] Standinge.

not

not go to haftely to it, for that is rafhneffe, nor yet make to much to do about it, for that is curiofity; the one foote muft not ftand to far from the other, leaft he ftoupe to much, which is unfemely, nor yet to nere together, leaft he ftande to ftreyghte uppe, for fo a man fhall neyther ufe his ftrength well, nor yet ftande ftedfaftlye.

The mean betwixt both muft be kept, a thinge more pleafaunt to behold when it is done, than eafy to be taught how it fhould be done.

To ¹ nocke well is the eafyeft pointe of all, and therein is no cunninge, but only diligente heede gevinge, to fet his fhafte neyther to hye nor to lowe, but even ftreight overwharte his bowe. Unconftant nockinge maketh a man leefe his lengthe. And befydes that, if the fhafte ende be hye, and the bowe-hand low, or contrarye, both the bowe is in jeopardye of breakinge, and the fhaft, if it be little, will ftart: if it be greate, it will hobble. Nocke the cocke fether upward alwayes, as I toulde you when I defcrybed the fether. And be fure alwayes that your ftringe flip not out of the nocke, for then all is in jeopardye of breakinge.

¹ Nockinge.

Drawinge

² Drawinge well is the beſt part of ſhootinge. Men in oulde time uſed other maner of drawinge than we do. They uſed to drawe lowe at the breaſt, to the right pappe, and no further; and this to be true is plaine in *Homer*, where he deſcrybeth *Pandarus* ſhootinge.

Up to the pap his ſtringe did he pull, his ſhafte to the hard heade.   Iliad 4.

The noble women of *Scythia* uſed the ſame faſhion of ſhootinge lowe at the breſt, and, becauſe theyr left pappe hindred theyr ſhooting at the lowſe, they cut it off when they were young, and therefore they be called, in lacking theyr pappe, *Amazones*. Nowe a daye, contrarywiſe, we drawe to the righte eare, and not to the pappe. Whether the old waye in drawinge lowe to the pappe, or the new way, to drawe alofte to the eare, be better, an excellent wryter in *Greeke*, called *Procopius*, doth ſaye his minde, ſhewinge that the olde faſhion in drawinge to the pappe was noughte of no pithe, and therefore, ſayth *Procopius*, is artillery diſprayſed in *Homer*, which calleth it ἀίδανος, *i. e.* weake, and able to do no good. Drawinge to the eare he prayſeth greatlye, whereby men ſhoote both ſtronger and longer: drawinge therefore to the eare is better than to drawe at the breſt. And one thinge

² Drawinge.

commeth into my remembraunce nowe, *Philologe,* when I speak of drawinge, that I never redde of other kinde of shootinge, than drawinge with a mans hande eyther to the breste or eare: this thing have I fought for in *Homer, Herodotus,* and *Plutarch,* and therefore I marveile how ³ crosbowe come first uppe, of the which, I am sure, a man shall find litle mention made on any good author. *Leo* the Emperour would have his fouldiours drawe quicklye in warre, for that maketh a shaft flye apace. In shootinge at the prickes, hastye and quicke drawinge is neyther sure nor yet comely. Therefore to drawe easely and uniformelye, that is for to say, not wagginge our hand, now upward, now downeward, but alwayes after one fashion, untill you come to the rigge or shouldringe of the heade, is best both for profite and seemelinesse. ⁴ Holdinge must not be longe, for it both putteth a bowe in jeopardye, and also marreth a mans shote; it must be so litle, that it may be perceyved better in a mans minde, when it is done, than seene with a mans eyes when it is in doinge. ⁵ Lowsinge must be much like. So quicke and harde, that it be without all girdes, so soft and gentle, that the shafte flye not as it were sent out of a bowe-case. The

³ Crosbowes. ⁴ Holdinge. ⁵ Lowsinge.

meane

meane betwixt both, which is perfite lowſinge, is not ſo harde to be folowed in ſhootinge as it is to be deſcrybed in teachinge. For cleane lowſinge, you muſt take heede of hitinge any thinge about you. And for the ſame purpoſe, *Leo* the Emperour would have all archers in warre to have theyr heades pouled, and theyr beardes ſhaven, leaſt the heere of theyr heads ſhould ſtoppe the ſighte of the eye, the heere of theyr beards hinder the courſe of the ſtringe. And theſe preceptes, I am ſure *Philologe*, if you folowe, in ſtanding, nocking, drawing, holding, and lowſing, ſhall bring you at the laſt to excellent fayre ſhootinge.   Phi. All theſe thinges, *Toxophile*, although I both now perceyve them thoroughlye, and alſo will remember them diligentlye: yet to-morrowe, or ſome other day when you have leyſure, we will go to the prickes, and put them by litle and litle in experience. For teachinge not folowed, doeth even as much good as bookes never looked upon. But now, ſeinge you have taughte me to ſhoote fayre, I pray you tell me ſomewhat, how I ſhould ſhoote neare, leaſt that proverbe might be ſayde juſtlye of me ſome time, *He ſhootes like a gentleman fayre and farre off.* Tox. He that can ſhoote fayre, lacketh nothing but ſhooting ſtreight, and keeping of a length,
whereof

whereof commeth hittinge of the marke, the ende both of shootinge, and also of this our communication. The handling of the wether and the marke, because they belonge to shootinge streight, and keping of a length, I will joyne them together, shewinge what thinges belonge to kepinge of a lengthe, and what to shootinge streight.

The greatest enemye of shooting is the [6] winde and the weather, whereby true kepinge a lengthe is chieflye hindered. If this thinge were not, men, by teachinge, might be brought to wonderfull neare shootinge. It is no marveile if the litle poore shaft, beinge sent alone so hye in the ayre, into a great rage of wether, one winde tossinge it that waye, another this waye, it is no marveile, I saye, though it leese the length, and misse that place where the shooter had thought to have found it. Greater matters than shootinge are under the rule and will of the weather, as in saylinge on the sea. And likewyse, as in saylinge, the chiefe point of a good master is to know the tokens of chaunge of wether, the course of the wyndes, that thereby he may the better come to the haven : even so the best propertye of a good shooter is to knowe the nature of

[6] Wynde and wether.

the

the windes, with him and againſt him, and thereby
he maye the nerer ſhoote at his marke. Wyſe
mayſters, when they cannot winne the beſt haven,
they are glad of the next : good ſhooters alſo, that
cannot when they woulde hit the marke, will labour to come as nigh as they can. All thinges in
this worlde be unperfite and unconſtant, therefore
let every man acknowledge his own weakneſſe in
all matters, greate and ſmall, weightye and merye,
and glorifye him, in whom onlye perfite perfiteneſſe is. But now, Sir, he that will at all adven-
tures uſe the ſeas, knowinge no more what is to
be done in a tempeſt than in a caulme, ſhall ſoone
become a merchaunt of ele ſkinnes ; ſo that ſhooter
which putteth no difference, but ſhooteth in all
alike, in roughe weather and fayre, ſhall alwayes
put his winninges in his eyes. Litle boates and
thinne boordes cannot endure the rage of a tempeſt.
Weake bowes, and light ſhaftes cannot ſtande in
a roughe wynde. And likewiſe, as a blind man,
which ſhould go to a place where he had never
beene afore, that hath but one ſtreight waye to it,
and of eyther ſyde hooles and pittes to fauie into,
now fauleth into this hoole, and then into that hoole,
and never cometh to his journey ende, but wan-
dereth alwayes here and there, further and further
of ;

of; so that archer which ignorantly shooteth, considering neyther fayre nor foule, standinge nor nockinge, fether nor head, drawinge nor lowsinge, nor any compasse, shall always shoote shorte and gone, wyde and farre off, and never come neare, excepte perchaunce he stumble sometime on the marke. For ignorance is nothing else but mere blindnesse.

A maister of a shippe first learneth to know the comminge of a tempest, the nature of it, and how to behave himselfe in it, eyther with chaunginge his course, or pulling downe his hye toppes and brode sayles, being glad to eschue as much of the wether as he can; even so a good archer will first, with diligent use and marking the weather, learne to knowe the nature of the winde, and, with wysedome, will measure in his minde, how much it will alter his shote, eyther in length kepinge, or else in streight shootinge, and so, with chaunging his standing, or taking another shaft, the which he knoweth perfitely to be fitter for his purpose, eyther because it is lower fethered, or else because it is of a better wynge, will so handle with discretion his shote, that he shall seem rather to have the wether under his rule, by good heede gevinge, than the wether to rule his shaft by any sodaine chaunginge.

Therefore,

Therefore, in shooting, there is as much difference betwixt an archer that is a good wether man,
and an other that knoweth and marketh nothinge,
as is betwixt a blinde man, and he that can see.

Thus, as concerninge the wether, a perfite archer must first learne to knowe the sure flighte of his
shaftes, that he may be bould alwayes to trust
them, than must he learne by daily experience all
maner of kindes of wether, the tokens of it, when
it will come, the nature of it when it is come ; the
diversity and altering of it when it chaungeth, the
decrease and diminishinge of it when it ceaseth.
Thirdlye, these thinges knowen, and every shote
diligently marked, then must a man compare alwayes the wether and his footinge together, and,
with discretion, measure them so, that whatsoever
the wether shall take away from his shote, the same
shall just footinge restore againe to his shote.   This
thinge well knowen, and discretelye handled in
shootinge, bringeth more profite and commendation and prayse to an archer, than any other thing
besydes.   He that would know perfectly the wind
and wether, must put differences betwixt times.
For diversity of time causeth diversity of wether,
as in the whole yeare. Spryng time, Sommer,
Faule

Faule of the leafe, and Winter: likewife in one daye, morninge, noontyde, afternoone, and eventyde, both alter the wether, and chaunge a mans bow with the ftrength of a man alfo. And to knowe that this is fo, is enough for a fhooter and artillerye, and not to fearche the caufe why it fhould be fo: which belongeth to a learned man and *Philofophie*. In confideringe the time of the year, a wyfe archer will folowe a good fhipman; in winter and roughe weather, fmall boates and litle pinkes forfake the feas: and at one time of the yeare no gallies come abrode: fo likewyfe weake archers, ufinge fmall and holowe fhaftes, with bowes of litle pithe, muft be content to geve place for a time. And this I do not fay, eyther to difcourage any weake fhooter: for likewife, as there is no fhippe better than galleys be, in a foft and caulme fea, fo no man fhooteth comlier, or nerer his marke, than fome weake archers do, in a fayre and cleare daye.

Thus every Archer muft know, not onlye what bowe and fhafte is fitteft for him to fhoote withall, but alfo what time and feafon is beft for him to fhoote in. And furely, in all other matters to, among all degrees of men, there is no man which doth any thinge eyther more difcretelye for his

E e   commendation,

commendation, or yet more profitable for his ad-
vauntage, than he which will knowe perfitely for
what matter, and for what tyme he is moft apt and
fitte. If men would go about matters which they
fhould do, and be fitte for, not fuche thinges which
wilfully they defyre, and yet be unfitte for, verelye
greater matters in the common wealth than fhootinge fhould be in better cafe than they be. This
ignorancye in men which knowe not for what time,
and to what thing they be fitte, caufeth fome wyfhe
to be riche, for whom it were better a greate deale
to be poore ; other to be medlinge in everye mans
matter, for whom it were more honeftye to be
quiete and ftill. Some to defyre to be in the court,
which be borne and be fitter rather for the carte.
Some to be maifters and rule other, which never
yet began to rule themfelves ; fome alwayes to iangle
and taulke, which rather fhoulde heare and kepe
filence. Some to teache, which rather fhould
learne. Some to be prieftes, which were fitter to
be clearkes. And this perverfe judgemente of the
worlde, when men meafure themfelves amiffe,
bringeth much diforder and great unfemelineffe to
the hole body of the common wealthe, as if a man
fhoulde weare his hoofe upon his heade, or a wo-
man go with a fworde and a buckler, everye man
                                        woulde

woulde take it as a greate uncumlineſſe, although it
be but a tryfle in reſpecte of the other.

This perverſe judgement of men hindereth nothing ſo muche as learninge, becauſe commonly
thoſe that be unfitteſt for learninge, be chieflye ſet
to learninge.   As if a man nowe a dayes have two
ſonnes, the one impotent, weke, ſicklye, liſpinge,
ſtutteringe, and ſtameringe, or havinge anye miſ-
ſhape in his bodye ; what doth the father of ſuche
one commonlye ſaye ?   This boye is fitte for nothinge elſe, but to ſet to learninge and make a prieſt
of, as who would ſay, the outcaſtes of the worlde,
having neyther countenance, tongue nor witte, (for
of a perverſe bodye commeth commonly a perverſe
minde) be good enoughe to make thoſe men of,
which ſhall be appointed to preache Gods holy
worde, and miniſter his bleſſed ſacramentes, beſydes other moſt weightye matters in the common
wealthe, put oft times, and worthely, to learned
mennes dyſcretion and charge ; when rather ſuch
an office, ſo highe in dignitye, ſo godly in admi-
niſtration, ſhould be committed to no man, which
ſhould not have a countenaunce full of comli-
neſſe, to allure good men, a bodye full of manly

authoritye

authoritye to * feare ill men, a witte apt for all
learninge, with tongue and voyce able to perfwade
all men. And althoughe fewe fuch men as thefe
can be founde in a common wealthe, yet furelye
a godlye difpofed man will both in his minde
thincke fit, and with all his ftudye labour to gette
fuch men as I fpeake of, or rather better, if better
can be gotten, for fuch an hye adminiftration,
which is moft properly appointed to Gods own
matters and bufineffes.

This perverfe judgemente of fathers, as concerninge the fitneffe and unfitneffe of theyr children,
caufeth the common wealth have manye unfit
myniﬅers : and feinge that myniﬅers be, as a manne
woulde fay, inﬅrumentes wherewith the common
wealth doth worke all her matters withall, I marveile how it chaunceth that a poore fhoomaker
hath fo much witte, that he will prepare no inﬅru-
mente for his fcience, neyther knyfe nor aule, nor
nothinge elfe which is not verye fit for him. The
common wealthe can be contente to take at a fonde
fathers hande the rifraffe of the worlde, to make
thofe inﬅrumentes of, wherewithall fhe fhoulde
woorke the hieﬅ matters under heaven. And

* To feare is to terrify.

furelye

furelye an aule of leade is not fo unprofitable in a
fhoo-makers fhoppe, as an unfit minifter, made of
groofe metell, is unfeemelye in the common wealthe.
Fathers in olde time, among the noble *Perfians*,
might not do with theyr children as they thought
good, but as the judgement of the common wealthe
alwayes thoughte beft. This faulte of fathers
bringeth manye a blot with it, to the great defor-
mitye of the common wealthe: and here furely I
can prayfe gentlewomen, which have alwayes at
hand theyr glaffes, to fee if any thinge be amiffe,
and fo will amende it, yet the common wealthe,
havinge the glaffe of knowledge in every mans
hande, doth fee fuche uncumlineffe in it, and yet
wincketh at it. This fault, and many fuch like,
might be foone wyped away, if fathers would beftowe theyr children on that thinge alwayes, whereunto nature hath ordayned them moft apt and fitte.
For if youth be grafted ftreighte, and not awrye,
the hole common wealthe will floryfhe thereafter.
When this is done, thenne mufte every man beginne
to be more readye to amende himfelfe, than to
checke another, meafuringe theyr matters with that
wyfe proverbe of *Apollo*, *Knowe thyfelfe*: that is to
faye, learne to knowe what thou art able, fitte, and
apte unto, and folowe that. This thinge fhould
                                                    be

be both cumlye to the common wealthe, and moſte
profitable for everye one, as doth appeare verye
well in all wyſe mennes deedes, and ſpeciallye (to
turne to our communication againe) in ſhootinge,
where wyſe archers have alwayes theyr inſtrumentes fitte for theyr ſtrength, and wayte evermore ſuch time and wether as is moſt agreeable to
theyr gere. Therefore, if the wether be to ſore, and
unfitte for your ſhootinge, leave off for that daye,
and wayte a better ſeaſon. For he is a foole that will
not go whom neceſſitye dryveth. PHI. This
communication of yours pleaſed me ſo well, *Toxophile*, that ſurelye I was not haſtye to call you to
deſcrybe forth the wether, but with all my hart
would have ſuffered you yet to have ſtande longer
in this matter. For theſe thinges touched of you
by chaunce, and by the waye, be farre above the
matter itſelfe, by whoſe occaſion the other were
brought in. TOX. Weightye matters they be
indeede, and fitte both in another place to be ſpoken,
and of an other man than I am to be handled.
And, becauſe meane men muſt meddle with meane
matters, I will go forwarde in deſcrybinge the wether as concerninge ſhootinge : and, as I toulde you
before, in the hole yere, Springe-time, Sommer,
Faule of the leafe, and Winter : and in one daye,
Morninge,

Morninge, Noonetime, Afternoone, and Eventyde, altereth the courſe of the wether, the pyth
of the bowe, the ſtrength of the man. And in
everye one of theſe tymes, the wether altereth, as
ſometime windy, ſometime caulme, ſometime clou-
dye, ſometime cleare, ſometime hot, ſometime
coulde, the wynde ſometime moiſtye and thicke,
ſometime drye and ſmoothe. A litle wynd in a
moiſtye day ſtoppeth a ſhafte more than a good
whyſkynge wynde in a cleare daye. Yea, and I
have ſeene when there hath bene no wynde at all,
the ayre ſo miſtye and thicke, that both the markes
have bene wonderfull great. And ones, when the
plague was in *Cambrige*, the * downe wynd twelve
ſcore marke for the ſpace of three weekes was thir-
teen ſcore and a half, and into the wynd, being
not very great, a great deale above fourteen ſcore.

The wynde is ſometime plaine up and downe,
which is commonlye moſt certaine, and requireth
leaſt knowledge, wherein a meane ſhooter, with
meane geare, if he can ſhoote home, may make
beſt ſhift. A ſyde wynd tryeth an archer and good
gere very much. Sometime it bloweth aloft, ſometime hard by the ground ; ſometime it bloweth by

* The downe wind, &c. This paſſage we do not fully underſtand.

blaſtes,

blaftes, and sometime it continueth all in one;
sometime full syde wynd, sometime quarter with
him, and more; and likewise againft him, as a
man with cafting up light grafle, or elfe, if he take
good heede, fhall fenfiblye learne by experience.
To fee the wynd, with a mans eyes, it is unpoffible,
the nature of it is fo fine, and fubtile, yet this experience of the wynd had I ones myfelfe, and that
was in the great fnowe that fell four yeares agoo.
I rode in the hye way betwixt *Topcliffe* upon *Swale*
and *Borowbridge*, the way being fomewhat troden
afore, by waye fayringe men; the fieldes on both
fides were playne, and laye almoft yeard deep with
fnowe, the night before had bene a litle frofte, fo
that the fnowe was harde, and crufted above; that
morninge the funne fhone bright and cleare, the
wynd was whiftling aloft, and fharpe, according to
the time of the yeare; the fnow in the hye waye
laye lowfe and troden with horfe feete; fo as the
wynd blewe, it toke the lowfe fnowe with it, and
made it fo flide upon the fnowe in the fielde, which
was harde and crufted by reafon of the froft over
nighte, that thereby I might fee very well the hole
nature of the wynde as it blewe that daye. And I
had a greate delyte and pleafure to marke it, which
maketh me now farre better to remember it. Sometime

time the wynde would be not paſt two yardes
brode, and ſo it would cary the ſnowe as farre as I
could ſee. Another time the ſnowe would blowe
over half the fielde at ones. Sometime the ſnowe
would tumble ſoftlye, by and by it would flye
the wonderful faſt. And this I perceyved alſo, that
wynde goeth by ſtreames, and not hole together.
For I ſhould ſee one ſtreame within a ſcore on
me, then the ſpace of two ſcore, no ſnowe would
ſtyre, but, after ſo much quantitye of grounde,
on other ſtreame of ſnowe, at the ſame very tyme,
ſhould be caryed likewyſe, but not equallye, for
the one would ſtande ſtyll, when the other flewe
apace, and ſo continue ſometime ſwiftlyer, ſometime ſlowlyer, ſometime broder, ſometime nar-
rower, as far as I could ſee. Nor it flewe not
ſtreighte, but ſometime it crooked this way,
ſometime that waye, and ſometime it ran round
about in a compaſſe. And ſometime the ſnowe
would be lyft cleane from the grounde up to the
ayre, and by and by it would be all clapt to the
ground, as though there had bene no wynd at all,
ſtreight way it would ryſe and flye againe. And
that which was the moſt marveile of all, at one
time two driftes of ſnowe flewe, the one oute of
the Weſt into the Eaſt, the other oute of the
North into the Eaſt. And I ſawe two wyndes,

F f

by

by reafon of the fnowe, the one croffe over the
other, as it had been two hye wayes. And,
againe, I fhould heare the winde blow in the
ayre, when nothing was ftyrred at the ground.
And when all was ftill where I rode, not verye
farre from me the fnow fhould be lifted wonderfullye. This experience made more marveile at
the nature of the wynde, that it made me cunninge in the knowledge of the wynde; but yet
thereby I learned perfitely that it is no marveile
at all though men in wynde leafe theyr length
in fhootinge, feeinge fo many ways the wynde is
fo variable in blowinge.

But feeing that a maifter of a fhyppe, be he
never fo cunninge, by the uncertainty of the
wynde, leefeth manye tymes both lyfe and goodes,
furelye it is no wonder, though a right good
archer, by the felfe fame wynde, fo variable in his
own nature, fo infenfible to our nature, leefe
many a fhote and game.

The more uncertaine and deceyvable the
wynde is, the more heede muft a wyfe archer
geve to know the gyles of it. He that doth
miftruft is feldome begyled. For although
thereby he fhall not attayne to that which is
beft,

beſt, yet by theſe meanes he ſhall at laſt avoyde
that which is worſt. Beſyde all theſe kindes of
wyndes, you muſt take heede if you ſee anye
cloude appeare, and gather by litle and litle
againſt you, or elſe, if a ſhower of rayne be lyke
to come upon you, for then both the dryvinge
of the wether and the thickinge of the ayre in-
creaſeth the marke, when, after the ſhower, all
thinges are contrarye cleare and caulme, and the
marke, for the moſt part, new to begin againe.
You muſt take heede alſo, if ever you ſhoote
where one of the markes, or bothe, ſtandes a little ſhort of a hye wall, for there you may be
eaſilye begyled. If you take graſſe and caſte it
up, to ſee howe the wynde ſtandes, many times
you ſhall ſuppoſe to ſhoote downe the wynde,
when you ſhoote cleane againſt the wynde. And
a good reaſon why. For the wynde which
commeth indeed againſt you, redoundeth backe
agayne at the waule, and whyrleth backe to the
pricke, and a litle farther, and then turneth
agayne, even as a vehement water doth againſt a
rocke, or an hye braye; which example of water,
as it is more ſenſible to a mans eyes, ſo it is never a whitte the truer than this of the wynde.
So that the graſſe caſte uppe ſhall flee that waye

F f 2   which

which indeede is the longer marke, and deceyve quicklye a shooter that is not ware of it.

This experience had I ones myselfe at *Norwytche* in the chappell field within the waules. And this way I used in shootinge at those markes. When I was in the mydde way betwixt the markes, which was an open place, there I toke a fethere, or a lyttle lighte grasse, and so, as well as I coulde, learned howe the wynde stoode; that done I went to the pricke as fast as I could, and, according as I had found the wynde when I was in the midde waye, so I was fayne then to be content to make the best of my shote that I could. Even such an other experience had I, in a maner, at *Yorke*, at the prickes lyinge betwixt the castle and *Ouse* syde. And although you smyle, *Philologe*, to heare me tell myne own fondnesse; yet, seeinge you will nedes have me teache you somewhat in shootinge, I must nedes sometime tell you of mine owne experience. And the better I may do so, because 7 *Hippocrates*, in teaching physicke, useth very muche the same waye. Take heede also when you shoote neare the sea coast, although you be two or three

7 Hippoc. de herb. un.

myles

myles from the fea, for there diligent marking
fhall efpye in the moft cleare daye wonderfull
chaunginge. The fame is to be confidered lyk-
wyfe by a ryver fyde, fpecially if it be ebbe and
flowe, where he that taketh diligente heede of
the tyde and wether, fhall lightlye take awaye
all that he fhooteth for. And thus, of the nature
of wyndes and wether, accordinge to my markinge, you have hearde, *Philologe* : and hereafter
you fhall marke farre mo yourfelfe, if you take
heede. And the wether thus marked, as I tolde
you afore, you muft take heede of your ftandinge, that thereby you may winne as much as
you fhall lofe by the wether. PHI. I fee well
it is no marveile though a man miffe many times
in fhootinge, feeinge the wether is fo unconftant
in blowinge, but yet there is one thinge which
many archers ufe, that fhall caufe a man have
leffe nede to marke the wether, and that is ame
gevinge. TOX. Of gevinge ame, I cannot tell
well what I fhould faye. For in a ftraunge place
it taketh away all occafion of foule game, which
is the onlye prayfe of it, yet, by my judgement,
it hindereth the knowledge of fhootinge, and
maketh men more negligent, they which is a
difprayfe. Though ame be geven, yet take
hede, for at another mans fhoote you cannot
well

well take ame, nor at your own neyther, because the wether will alter, even in a minute,
and at that one marke, and not at the other,
and trouble your shafte in the ayre, when you
shall perceive no wynde at the grounde, as I
myselfe have seen shaftes tumble alofte in a verye fayre daye. There may be a fault also in
drawinge or lowsing, and manye thinges mo,
which altogether are required to keepe a just
length. But, to go forewarde, the next point
after the markinge of your wether, is the taking
of your standing. And, in a syde wynde, you
must stande somewhat crosse into the wynde,
for so shall you shoote the surer. When you
have taken good footing, then must you loke at
your shafte, that no earth, nor weete, be left
upon it, for so should it leese the length. You
must loke at the head also, least it have had any
strype at the last shote. A strype upon a stone,
many times will both marre the head, croke the
shaft, and hurt the fether, whereof the least of
them all will cause a man leese his * strengthe.
For such thinges which chaunce every shoote,
manye archers use to have some place made in
theyr coate, fit for a litle fyle, a stone, a hunfysh

* Perhaps it should be length.

skin

skin, and a clothe to dreſſe the ſhaft fit againe at all needes. This muſt a man loke to ever when he taketh uppe his ſhafte. And the heade may be made to ſmoothe, which will cauſe it flye to farre: when your ſhafte is fitte, then muſt you take your bowe even in the middes, or els you you ſhall both leeſe your length, and put your bowe in jeopardye of breakinge. Nocking juſt is next, which is much of the ſame nature. Then drawe equallye, lowſe equally, with houldinge your hande ever of one height to kepe true com-paſſe. To loke at your ſhafte heade at the lowſe is the greateſt helpe to kepe a lengthe that can be, which thing yet hindereth excellente ſhootinge, becauſe a man cannot ſhoote ſtreight perfectlye excepte he loke at his marke; if I ſhould ſhoote at a line, and not at the marke, I would alwayes loke at my ſhafte ende: but of this thinge ſome what afterwarde. Nowe, if you marke the wether diligentlye, kepe your ſtandinge juſtlye, hould and nocke truely, drawe and lowſe equally, and kepe your compaſſe cer-tainlye, you ſhall never miſſe of your lengthe. PHI. Then there is nothing behinde to make me hit the marke, but only ſhooting ſtreight. Tox. No trulye. And firſt I will tell you what ſhiftes archers have founde to ſhoote ſtreight,

ſtreight, then what is the beſt way to ſhoote
ſtreight. As the wether belongeth ſpeciallye to
kepe a lengthe (yet a ſyde wynde belongeth alſo
to ſhoote ſtreight) even ſo the nature of the pricke
is to ſhoote ſtreighte. The lengthe or ſhortneſſe
of the marke is always under the rule of the
wether, yet ſomewhat there is in the marke,
worthie to be marked of an archer. If the
prickes ſtande on a ſtreighte plaine grounde,
they be the beſte to ſhoote at. If the marke
ſtande on a hill-ſyde, or the grounde be unequall
with pittes and turninge wayes betwixt the
markes, a mans eye ſhall thincke that to be
ſtreighte which is crooked: the experience of
this thinge is ſeen in paintinge, the cauſe of it
is known by learninge: and it is enough for an
archer to marke it, and take heede of it. The
chiefe cauſe whye men cannot ſhoot ſtreight, is
becauſe they loke at theyr ſhafte; and this faulte
commeth, becauſe a man is not taughte to ſhoote
when he is younge. If he learne to ſhoote by
himſelfe, he is afraide to pull the ſhaft through
the bowe, and therefore loketh alwayes at his
ſhaft; ill uſe confirmeth this fault as it doth
many mo. And men continue the longer in
this fault, becauſe it is ſo good to kepe a lengthe
withall: and yet to ſhoote ſtreighte, they have

invented

invented fome wayes to efpye a tree or a hill beyonde the marke, or els to have fome notable
thing betwixt the markes; and ones I faw a good
archer which did caft off his gere, and layed his
quiver with it, even in the mid waye betwixte
the prickes. Some thought he did it for fave-
guard of his gere: I fuppofe he did it to fhoote
ftreighte withall. Other men ufe to efpye fome
marke almoft a bowe wyde of the pricke, and
then go about to kepe himfelfe on the hand that
the pricke is on, which thinge how much good
it doth, a man will not believe, that doth not
prove it. Other, and thofe very good archers,
in drawinge, loke at the marke untill they come
almoft to the heade, then they loke at theyr
fhafte, but, at the verye lowfe, with a fecond
fight, they finde theyr marke againe. This waye,
and all other afore of me reherfed, are but fhiftes,
and not to be folowed in fhootinge ftreight. For
having a mans eye alwaye on his marke, is the
onlye waye to fhoote ftreighte, yea and, I fuppofe, fo redye and eafye a waye, if it be learned
in youth, and confirmed with ufe, that a man
fhall never miffe therein. Men doubt yet in
loking at the marke what way is beft, whether
betwixt the bowe and the ftringe, above or beneath his hande, and manye wayes mo: yet it

G g   maketh

maketh no greate matter which waye a man loke at his marke, if it be joyned with comelye ſhootinge. The diverſity of mens ſtanding and drawing cauſeth divers men loke at their marke divers wayes ; yet they all leade a mans hande to ſhoote ſtreight, if nothing els ſtoppe. So that cumlyneſſe is the only judge of beſt lokinge at the marke. Some men wonder whye, in caſtinge a mans eye at the marke, the hande ſhould go ſtreighte : ſurelye if he conſidered the nature of a mans eye, he would not wonder at it : for this I am certain of, that no ſervaunt to his maiſter, no childe to his father, is ſo obedient, as everye joynte and peece of the bodye is to do whatſoever the eye biddes. The eye is the guide, the ruler and the ſuccourer of all the other partes. The hande, the foote, and other members, dare do nothinge without the eye, as doth appear on the night and darcke corners. The eye is the very tongue wherewith witte and reaſon doth ſpeake to everye parte of the bodye, and the witte doth not ſo ſoon ſignifye a thinge by the eye, as every part is redye to folowe, or rather prevent the biddinge of the eye. This is plaine in manye thinges, but moſt evident in fence and feighting, as I have heard men ſaye. There everye parte ſtandinge in feare to have a

blowe,

blowe, runnes to the eye for helpe, as younge
children do to the mother; the foote, the hande,
and all wayteth upon the eye. If the eye bid
the hande eyther bear of or smite, or the foote
eyther go forward, or backward, it doth so; and
that which is moſt wonder of all, the one man
lokinge ſtedfaſtly at the other mans eye, and not
at his hande, will, even as it were, rede in his
eye where he purpoſeth to ſmyte next, for the
eye is nothing els but a certaine window for wit
to ſhoote out her heade at.

This wonderfull worke of God in makinge all
the members ſo obedient to the eye, is a pleaſant
thinge to remember and loke upon; therefore an
archer may be ſure, in learninge to loke at his
marke when he is younge, alwayes to ſhoote
ſtreight. The thinges that hinder a man which
loketh at his marke, to ſhoote ſtreight, be theſe:
a ſyde winde, a bowe eyther to ſtronge, or els to
weake, an ill arme, when a fether runneth on
the bowe to much, a bigge breſted ſhafte, for
him that ſhooteth under hande, becauſe it will
hobble; a litle breſted ſhafte for him that
ſhooteth above the hande, becauſe it will ſtarte;
a payre of windinge prickes, and many other
thinges mo, which you ſhall marke yourſelfe,
and

and as ye know them, ſo learne to amende
them. If a man would leave to loke at his ſhaft,
and learne to loke at his marke, he maye uſe
this waye, which a good ſhooter told me ones
that he did. Let him take his bowe on the night,
and ſhoot at two lightes, and there he ſhall be
compelled to looke alwayes at his marke, and
never at his ſhafte: this thinge, ones or twiſe
uſed, will cauſe him forſake loking at his ſhafte.
Yet let him take heede of ſetting his ſhafte in
the bowe.

Thus, *Philologe*, to ſhoote ſtreight is the leaſt
maiſterye of all, if a man order himſelfe thereafter in his youthe. And as for kepinge a
length, I am ſure, the rules which I gave you
will never deceyve you; ſo that there ſhall lacke
nothing, eyther of hittinge the marke alwayes,
or els verye neare ſhootinge, except the faulte
be onlye in youre owne ſelfe, which may come
two wayes, eyther in having a fainte harte, or
courage, or els in ſufferinge yourſelfe overmuch
to be ledde with affeſtion: if a mans minde
fayle him, the bodye, which is ruled by the
minde, can never do his dutye, if lacke of courage were not, men might do mo maiſtries than
they

they do, as doth appeare in leapinge and vault-
inge.

All affections, and especiallye anger, hurteth
both minde and body. The minde is blinde
thereby, and, if the minde be blinde, it cannot
rule the bodye arighte. The bodye, both bloude
and bone, as they saye, is brought out of his
right course by anger: whereby a man lacketh
his righte strength, and therefore cannot shoote
well. If these thinges be avoyded (whereof I
will speake no more, both because they belonge
not properlye to shootinge, and also you can
teache me better in them than I you) and all the
preceptes which I have given you diligentlye
marked, no doubte ye shall shoote as well as
ever man did yet, by the grace of God.

This communication handled of me, *Philologe*,
as I know well not perfitelye, yet, as I suppose
trulye, you must take it in good worthe, wherein,
if divers thinges do not altogether please you,
thancke your selfe, which woulde have me rather
faulte in mere follye, to take that thinge in
hande, which I was not able for to perfourme;
than by any honest shamefastnesse with-saye your
request and minde, which I knowe well I have
not

not fatisfyed. But yet I will thincke this labour of myne the better beftowed, if to-morrowe, or fome other daye when you have leyfure, you will fpende as much time with me here in this fame place, in entreating the queftion *De origine animæ*, and the joyninge of it with the bodye, that I maye knowe howe farre *Plato*, *Ariftotle*, and the *Stoycians* have waded in it.

PHI. Howe you have handled this matter, *Toxophile*, I maye not well tell you myfelfe now, but, for your gentleneffe and good will towardes learninge and fhootinge, I will be content to fhewe you anye pleafure whenfoever you will ; and now the funne is downe, therefore, if it pleafe you, we will go home and drincke in my chamber, and there I will tell vou plainlye what I thincke of this communication, and alfo what daye we will appointe, at your requeft, for the other matter to meete here againe.

THE END OF THE SCHOLE OF SHOOTINGE.

THE

TABLE

OF THE

FIRST BOOKE

OF THE

SCHOLE of SHOOTINGE.

THE
TABLE
OF THE
SECONDE BOOKE
OF THE
SCHOLE of SHOOTINGE.